THE FOOTPRINTS

MOHAMMAD AHSAN

ANAM ZAKARIA is a twenty-seven-year-old development professional, educationist and researcher based in Pakistan. She has an academic background in international development from McGill University and started off her career with the Citizens Archive of Pakistan (CAP) in 2010. She led their Oral History Project, Exchange-for-Change Project and School and College Outreach Tours in Lahore and Islamabad, collecting narratives of the first and second generations of Pakistanis, opening communication channels between schoolchildren in India and Pakistan and Pakistan and USA. She currently works in the education sector with the Association for the Development of Pakistan. Anam is also a teacher of development studies, and a student of psychotherapy, with a special interest in trauma and healing in conflict zones. She was born and brought up in Lahore and currently resides in Islamabad with her husband. This is her first book.

ADVANCE PRAISE FOR THE BOOK

'Told with compassion, curiosity and sometimes gentle humour, these Partition accounts give life to the dry documents of history; they remind us of how much there is to be learned from the lived experiences of those caught in its sweep.'—Urvashi Butalia, author of *The Other Side of Silence: Voices from the Partition of India*, and *Partition: The Long Shadow*

'Drawing upon rich layers of oral histories, archives and fast fading voices, Anam Zakaria paints a rather unforgettable image of what the earlier generations underwent, and in some cases continue to do. It is now for the third-generation Pakistanis and Indians to undo the toxic past and ensure that it doesn't repeat itself. This is why *The Footprints of Partition* is such an essential book of the future.'—Raza Rumi, journalist and author of *Delhi by Heart*

'A moving, inspiring and thoughtful first-person account of a young woman's process of "unlearning" about "the enemy" and learning to embrace and accept the "other" as fellow human beings. The process involves a rich and varied series of experiences that Anam Zakaria shares openly with readers, lightly interspersed with historical context and her own insightful analyses.'—Beena Sarwar, writer and documentary filmmaker

'Anam's effort in writing this book has been painstaking, sensitive, realistic, constructive and necessary. She has performed a distinct service.'—Rajmohan Gandhi, biographer and journalist

'Anam Zakaria probes residue of the horrific events of '47, through sensitively conducted conversations. She sifts through memories, long supressed or glossed over. These vastly varied chronicles are compelling, each in its own way. They help to piece togther a people's history, often at odds with the grand narratives of the state.'—Salima Hashmi, writer and artist

'Anam Zakaria's book on Partition brings a kind of freshness and *insaniyat* to our understanding of the event. It is about young people in Pakistan trying to break free from inherited prejudices, and longing to find, like many in India and elsewhere, secular spaces of justice and peace in the near future. We need, urgently, a new politics of hope.'—Dr Alok Bhalla, author of *Stories about the Partition of India* and *Partition Dialogues*

THE FOOTPRINTS OF PARTITION

Narratives of Four Generations of
Pakistanis and Indians

ANAM ZAKARIA

HarperCollins *Publishers* India

First published in India in 2015 by
HarperCollins *Publishers* India

Copyright © Anam Zakaria 2015

P-ISBN: 978-93-5136-551-8
E-IBSN: 978-93-5136-552-5

2 4 6 8 10 9 7 5 3 1

Anam Zakaria asserts the moral right to be identified
as the author of this work.

The views and opinions expressed in this book are the author's own
and the facts are as reported by her, and the publishers
are not in any way liable for the same.

HarperCollins *Publishers*
A-75, Sector 57, Noida, Uttar Pradesh 201301, India
1 London Bridge Street, London SE1 9GF, United Kingdom
Hazelton Lanes, 55 Avenue Road, Suite 2900, Toronto, Ontario M5R 3L2
and 1995 Markham Road, Scarborough, Ontario M1B 5M8, Canada
25 Ryde Road, Pymble, Sydney, NSW 2073, Australia
195 Broadway, New York, NY 10007, USA

Typeset in 12/16 Requiem Text-HTF at
SÜRYA, New Delhi

Printed and bound at
Thomson Press (India) Ltd.

To Muhammad Rauf and the countless other Indians and Pakistanis who have died with the aching desire to cross the border and reconnect with the homes and lives they left behind in 1947

CONTENTS

ACKNOWLEDGEMENTS

So many people have been a part of this journey, so many have been responsible for making this happen. However, perhaps the most important are those whose stories I explored during my research. For, without them, there would be no book. I would like to express my gratitude to each person who has allowed me to record his or her story; I realize how painful it has been for some of them to go down memory lane with me. As a writer, the most difficult job has been to do justice to their stories. To bring to light the emotions, the experiences that have shaped their lives. I do know that every word they have shared has become an integral part of me. I am no longer the person I was before I travelled with them through their past and present.

And now to the people who may not have necessarily made it to the pages of this book but are fundamental to its birth: Abu, I write because you write, not as well nor as profusely but I think I love it as much as you do. I also read because you read; because you pushed me to pick up books instead of the TV remote throughout my childhood. Today, these are two of my greatest passions and I am incomplete without them, as I am incomplete without you. Ami, I have thought the hardest of how to thank you and I still don't know how. I don't remember a moment in my life when you haven't been there for me, with your unwavering belief and confidence. You are my rock. Haroon, thank you for reading each word, for always pushing me to go the extra mile and standing by me as I attempt to leap forward; I couldn't have done it without you. Nano, your vivid imagination and your extraordinary storytelling skills have been instrumental in opening me up to a world of writing. Nana, my anchor, my mentor, my confidant—I miss you so much. Chintan Girish Modi: thank you for inspiring me to write this book. Sharmeen Obaid-Chinoy and Swaleha Alam Shahzada: for all the encouragement and facilitation, every step of the way. My sisters Lyla, Mehreen, Jasmyn, Amal and Natasha: for always standing by me. My friends and colleagues—Iqbal Qaiser, Owais Rana, Asma Asif, Hina Mansoor, Mariam Javed, Abrar Ali, Alizeh Khalid, Asiya Shoaib, Ammar Khalid, Kavita Anand and Manjri Sewak: for the enormous support during the writing process. My agent Kanishka Gupta and Writer's Side Agency, for representing me and linking me to one of the best publishers in India; you have the power to make dreams come true. My publisher Karthika V.K. and editor Amit Agarwal, thank you for believing in this book and for your confidence in a first-time author. Amit, I have realized how crucial an editor is to the writing process and I thank you wholeheartedly for making this book readable.

Finally, I would like to acknowledge the Citizens Archive of Pakistan (CAP) for allowing me to use experiences from two CAP-sponsored trips to India in 2012 and for using its Oral History Project archive to supplement research. Of course, I alone am responsible, and not CAP, for the way the research has been interpreted or presented in this book.

PROLOGUE

I remember sitting squeezed at the back of a small silver Cuore, on the way back to Lahore from Sahiwal, when the idea of writing this book struck me. I turned towards my then fiancé, Haroon, and told him I had heard the most beautiful story the afternoon before; it was one that had to be documented. The story was of a Pakistani man in his seventies, desperately longing to go visit his home in Amritsar that he had left behind as a child at Partition. He told me that once he had come close to visiting when he was travelling to Qadian for a religious procession alongside other members of the Ahmadiyya community. He had stood at the Wagah border and then passed through Amritsar in a bus, trying to soak in as much as he could. But he couldn't get off; he couldn't visit his home despite being so near. Pakistan and India only issue city visas; his was limited to Qadian and his home wasn't in the allowed perimeters. He had cried while narrating the incident, and in a choked voice he told me it was his dying wish to be able to see his neighbourhood one last time. It remained just a wish, for he passed away a few months later.

At this time I was heading the Oral History Project for the Citizens Archive of Pakistan (CAP) in Lahore and Islamabad. CAP is a non-profit organization dedicated to cultural and historic preservation of Pakistan. As part of their Oral History Project team, conducting Partition interviews had become my source of bread and butter. Over a period of almost three years, I conducted 600 such in-depth interviews (including follow-ups)—both for CAP and independently—mostly in and around Lahore and across different socio-economic classes. The narratives, as expected, were very often imprinted with horrific memories of torture, rape, lootings, kidnappings, death and displacement. These bloody accounts were similar to the ones I had heard from my own maternal grandmother, who served at Lahore's largest refugee camp at Walton. They were also similar to what I had read in my history textbooks as a student.

Some people were open to readily sharing, others more reluctant; sometimes I had to return again and again before people were willing to reopen that chapter of their lives with me, and other times the very first interview ran for hours and hours, one horror story rolling in after the other. Some cried during the interviews, others spoke about losing entire families without as much as a tremble.

However, what also started to come forth alongside these narratives were other experiences, experiences that I was unfamiliar with, experiences that I had not read or heard anywhere before. And even if they had been mentioned by my grandparents or others, in this anecdote or that, they remained so insignificant in my larger framework and understanding of history that I brushed them away without much thought. These were stories of joint festivities, of sending *mithai* (sweets) to each other's homes at Diwali and Eid before Partition. Stories of school friends, stories of neighbours who were more like family, stories of rescue rather than vengeance at Partition.

Stories of post-Partition divided families, of wanting to travel across the border, of the desire to visit their abandoned homes and friends.

One such recent narration had moved me. Viqar, who was thirteen at Partition, had left behind his family's 350-year-old *haveli* in India to come to Pakistan. But as Viqar told me, the relations his family held with Meerut for over three centuries could not be eradicated overnight. 'Even when I go back now all these years later, they always embrace me. I remember the first time I visited Meerut again was in 1956, almost ten years after Partition. My neighbours and friends clung to me and began weeping. The women gathered around me too. They were crying and asking for my mother and sisters. These were my people, my home. We had lived together for so long. How could we forget one another?'

Viqar told me that even today, half of his family income comes from his mango orchards in Meerut. It is looked after by his neighbours and friends, many of whom are Hindus and Sikhs.

Some would rightly attribute such recollections to an idealization of the past, of the lost days becoming greener than they were. In one of the largest studies conducted on the political psychology of Partition, political psychologist Ashis Nandy makes note of this. 'There is utopianism, or repeated references to life in undivided India as flawless, rosy in every respect, a utopia of nostalgia. Most respondents see nothing wrong with their life before Partition. It was the division of the country that started their problems, before 1947 they had nothing to worry about . . . Sardar Vasudev Singh Bindra, a refugee from Rawalpindi [says]: "There was nothing wrong with our life there. We had everything, land, respect in the community, prosperity. Only after 1947 we suddenly had nothing . . ."[1]

Historical research and facts show that fault lines existed prior to Partition as well. Riots and arguments would break out between different communities—albeit as isolated events rather than the large-scale chaotic violence that Partition brought—and there were many instances of oppression and discrimination. However, as Viqar stated, even when relationships became tense, it was not possible to completely break away from the other. The multicultural dynamics of the pre-Partition years were different, with almost a co-dependence of one community on the other. The religious and cultural identities that became crystalized at Partition were far more diluted and fluid in the preceding years. Rajmohan Gandhi explains this in his writing: 'Normal life usually prevailed on the ground, and cordial exchanges took place during festivals, though the century-old tension between purity of belief and purity of birth was present even in the 1930s and 1940s. If this tension remained part of Punjab's climate, the Punjabis' ability to put it to one side was a stronger part.'[2]

It is my understanding that Partition was too complex an event and the pre-Partition years too multilayered to be neatly packed into categories of hate or friendship, rescue or violence. This is especially so because it was often the same people who narrated both, stories of bonds and loss, of comradeship and hostility, from different instances of their lives. The dichotomy between good and bad, between violence and harmony, was

---

[1]Ghose, Sagarika, *The Partition Psychosis*. http://www.outlookindia.com/article/The-Partition-Psychosis/204034 (last accessed: 24 November 2014).

[2]Gandhi, Rajmohan, *Punjab: A History from Aurangzeb to Mountbatten*. p.365.

blurred for many of them. Thus, it is not my job to testify which versions of history, the dark or the rosy, are the correct ones. Instead, Partition stories need to be looked at as shades on a spectrum and understood as experiences, each unique to the storyteller. How they recollect, how and what they choose to remember, depends on their own individual process, and for me it is as important as any historical fact.

What was of personal interest during these interviews then, was that if such recollections existed, of happier days and intercommunal bonds both before and after Partition, why had they not been shared more often and why was I only hearing of them now? At this time—about five years ago—I was a fresh twenty-two-year-old university graduate and was only beginning my journey of exploring my own history, both as a family and as a nation. The idea that my learning until now had been filtered was both new and distressing for me.

I began to realize that often such stories would be uttered casually, as a long pause in larger narratives of violence and displacement. One reason for this was how people remembered and recalled Partition, which I will address in a moment. The other was because I too had become a selective listener. Being a product of a security state that views its neighbours, especially the eastern one, with great suspicion and animosity, where autorickshaws publicly carry slogans of 'Bharat se rishta kya? Nafrat ka, intiqam ka!' (What is our relationship with India, but that of hatred and revenge), I could not quite reconcile that with the fact that Partition survivors would want to revisit the horrific past, that they would want to go back to see their friends and homes, and that they could still consider them as friends and see the other country as home in the first place. Wasn't the whole reason that Pakistan was created was to stay away from 'them' and what 'they' had done to 'us'? After all, we had fought major wars with India, the Kashmir issue had been burning while I was growing up in the 1990s and I was often told by my schoolteachers and even my own grandmother that Hindus were treacherous and mischievous people; that they would discriminate against Muslims and abuse Islam. I was also told that India was a major player in creating the current instability in Pakistan. Media channels further reiterated this line of thought by endorsing India as an archrival, an enemy of Islamabad. Even as I write this, conflict at the border has heightened. Another headline states how India has been accused of violating the Indus water treaty.

Thus, as a listener, I was tuning in and out unconsciously. When accounts would roll in of how Muslims were treated like untouchables, of how there were separate Muslim and Hindu water fountains in schools, of how Muslim women only had a choice between being raped or drowning in already overcrowded wells, I would become ever attentive. These stories fit into my expectations of Partition. The other ones seemed like an anomaly, perhaps just experiences of a handful, not important enough to engage with.

It was only when I spoke to the man in Sahiwal that something switched on within me. His tears, his cracking voice, his trembling hands pushed me to think about his reality. It also pushed me to question my listening skills, my own prejudices as a researcher. I started going back to the interviews—and later to the interviewees—I had conducted before Sahiwal and was surprised how many other interviewees like Viqar had off-handedly mentioned the name of a Hindu or Sikh friend prior to Partition, of how a description of Lahore was incomplete without the mention of Diwali celebrations at Laxmi Chowk. In the interviews I conducted from that day onwards, I became ever conscious of this. Slowly, the interviewees and I began to explore the hidden layers of narratives they held within. At the slightest encouragement they began to offer countless stories of the friends they had lost, of how some had had a chance to reconnect while others ached with longing to do the same. My own grandmother opened up to me as she had not done with anyone in the family. In the middle of the brutal stories from refugee camps came in stories of her Hindu friends Rajeshvari and Uma, of how my nani's sister was saved by a Sikh family, of how her baby sister's nickname was kept by her father's Sikh friend. These were stories no one in my family had heard; had I not probed, they would have passed away with my grandmother, as must have countless other tales millions of grandparents held deeply seated in their hearts since 1947.

Memory over time becomes selective, it filters out information, it gets influenced by metanarratives, by tragic life experiences. When something as huge and traumatic as Partition happens, other incidents and memories recede to the background. This is what I have found in many people that I have interviewed. It is often with probing that other stories and realities, that are less tragic, come to the forefront. In her book, *Since 1947: Partition Narratives among Punjabi Migrants of Delhi* (OUP 2007), Ravinder Kaur shows how private and collective memories often influence each other and how meta- and micronarratives often intertwine and profoundly impact individual experiences and memory. Reviewing her work, Urvashi Butalia writes how 'Partition refugees often personalize stories of general violence and trauma, telling and feeling them to be their own, and marking the shifts in political

climate, location, as felt, personal things.'³ For many of the
people I interviewed, living in a country where TV
programmes, education curriculums, political campaigns and
mainstream discourse all reinforce the bloodshed of Partition
and the need for separation, personal memories also begin to
absorb these narratives as their own, making it difficult to
decipher between personal tragedies and collective
understandings of the past, shaped by multiple and often
external forces. It is then not a surprise that the violent stories
were at the tip of the tongue for many people I spoke to
whereas other ones, of bonds and desires, often had to be
pushed and prodded for.

While hearing these stories, a slow process of unlearning
began to take place in me. While my education and the
mainstream discourse in and around me had made me believe
that the dark accounts were the only accounts of history, that
these were the only experiences my ancestors had had, I began
to learn that the pre-Partition days were far more complex.
There were no blacks and whites about good Muslims and bad
Hindus and Sikhs, there were no stark dichotomies of
treacherous infidels and innocent believers. These were
individuals, children, men and women. These were people
who had lived together for generations. They remembered the
turmoil of the Partition years but many also terribly ached to
meet their Hindu and Sikh friends who had been left behind.
There was nostalgia, a longing to reconnect. This in no way
discounted the madness of Partition but what was important
was that if such recollections existed, they should have been

---

³Butalia, Urvashi, 'Memory, Lived and Forgotten', *The Financial Express*,
1 April 2007.

shared and re-told alongside other stories of Partition, which were far darker and bloodier. And what I increasingly began to find was that these stories were missing, not just from my life but also from those of thousands of other Pakistanis, both older and younger. And the result was deep mistrust and animosity breeding in the Pakistani youth towards the 'other'. And even where they had been shared, it seemed like the jingoistic narratives predominant in society had stood in the way—and, in many cases, hijacked a more nuanced and holistic understanding of the past. This became even more obvious to me when CAP launched its Exchange-for-Change programme in 2010.

Heading it in Lahore and Islamabad for almost three years, I was meant to connect five thousand schoolchildren—aged between ten and fourteen—in India and Pakistan through letters, photographs, oral histories and finally, a physical exchange. The idea behind the project was to encourage cross-culture communication and give students on both sides of the border a clearer understanding of their shared history, culture and lifestyles. A major goal of the project was also to challenge negative stereotypes the young generations held of the 'other' as a result of over six decades of wars and conflicts, animosity, media propaganda and limited people-to-people contact. It was in these workshops in Pakistan that I realized that the notion I had of Partition and India was mirrored in these students' perspectives.

Thinking back, perhaps it was strange that CAP chose me to head this exchange for I had my own stereotypes about 'them'. However, given that I had studied with many Indian students for three years in Canada while completing my undergraduate degree meant that my opinions had become less hardline and what one may call more forward-looking; our history was bloody but one couldn't blame all Indians for what had happened just as one could not blame every German for the holocaust. We had to forget the past and move forward. But these students, belonging to low- to upper-middle-income schools, had not had the same privilege to interact with Indians. As in my childhood, they too had only heard stories about enmity, rivalry and revenge. For many of them, to contemplate being friends or even writing a letter to an Indian was nothing less than a sin. Indians had murdered Muslims, tortured their ancestors and snatched away their homes. What need was there to talk to such an enemy? They detested the Indians their own grandparents had grown up amongst; there was no room for dialogue, no need to cross over.

Conversing with the Partition generation on one hand and these young students on the other, the disconnect between the two kept glaring back at me. Why was it that I was finding so many children, who were born over five decades after Partition, holding so much bitterness? When many of their forefathers had spent so many fond days amidst their Hindu and Sikh friends, when many had tried desperately to cross the border to see their homes one more time, why were the younger generations so unwilling to talk, so unwilling to interact with the 'other'? Was it because for many of their grandparents and great-grandparents, the happier and peaceful memories were often seated in the subconscious and they simply had never shared them, as my grandmother hadn't? Was it because our younger generations were learning a selected and censored version of history through textbooks and media propaganda and had a filtered understanding of 1947, as I did? And if this was the case, was there a way to revive stories from the first generation, who served as walking, talking, living history?

It was these very questions that pushed me to research and write this book. Through it I have attempted to research how Partition and the 'other' are understood through the different generations and what changes, if any, there have been in this understanding over the years. I am very aware that the post-Partition generation is not one homogenous group; those in their fifties and sixties and those who are barely teenagers cannot be thrown into one monolithic cluster. And even between similar age groups, there are variances and exceptions. The experience of their families at Partition, the way oral histories have been narrated, their exposure to liberal education, their personal experiences and insights and travel all have enomormous influence on their understanding of history and attitude towards the 'other'.

The book includes seventeen long interviews in total, covering four generations of Pakistanis, and a few Indians. While there is no clear distinction between where one generation begins and the other ends, for the sake of this book, I have divided the people I have interviewed into four groups. The first generation includes people like my grandmother, who was in her early twenties at Partition. These individuals are the Partition survivors, who were old enough in 1947 to have strong recollections of the past. They also spent many years in the undivided subcontinent. The next generation is that of my mother—either very young at Partition or born right after. I would consider myself, born in the 1980s as the third generation whereas the young children today, those who are still in school, are the upcoming fourth generation.

These seventeen interviewees were selected in particular because each of them represents a different set of experiences, backgrounds and age groups, which are critical in order to understand the varying perspectives regarding Partition and India in Pakistan. For instance, I have particularly selected some interviewees who have had a chance to work on the other side of the border in different professional capacities— be it sportsmen or choreographers—as their access to India is instrumental in shaping their memories and opinions about the 'other'. At the same time, I also found it essential to add other narratives, for instance, those of army officials and their children who have seen and felt the repercussions of the conflicted relationship with India first-hand. Stories of ordinary people, divided from family members and homes, have been included to gain a glimpse into the personal stories and experiences of Partition. I have also included stories of young Pakistanis, growing up decades after Partition. Within these young Pakistanis, one finds many voices—of those who are ready to move on and build fresh relationships with Indians and those who are unable to do so—depending on their education, exposure and family histories.

Of these seventeen interviewees, the names of six have been changed upon their request. The reason stated by the interviewees was simply that they did not feel comfortable openly sharing their views. Respecting their decision, in each chapter where a name has been altered, the reader is informed of it in parentheses.

My research is limited to its sample size and geography (largely Lahore and nearby cities like Sahiwal and Kasur), so I will not make any tall claims that these narratives are the only truth or that they apply to all Pakistanis. Regional differences and varied historical realities play a critical role in shaping perceptions. I also fully understand the limitations of using the oral history technique for research. Here I must also mention that by predominantly focusing on those stories that show how the Partition generation still has a longing for their friends and homes across the border or by highlighting how they spent many happy afternoons among Hindu and Sikh friends prior to 1947, I am not rejecting the insanity of Partition or the conflicts that preceded the event. Nor am I generalizing that everyone in the Partition generation had fond stories to tell or that all of them even wanted to revisit 1947. Many chose to put those years aside, many never wanted to reopen that chapter of their lives. I am, however, deliberately sharing these stories because I believe they are valid as any other stories or facts that have so far been documented, and are crucial for the younger generations to explore, for as we lose the Partition survivors and move further and further away from 1947, we are at risk of absorbing an increasingly rigid and myopic narrative of Partition in its entirety. The repercussions of this, needless to say, are grave.

It must also be mentioned that it is unfortunate that I was unable to conduct detailed research in India. Funding constraints, visa issues and the fact that I had a full-time job while researching and writing this book are the prime reasons for this. While I have been fortunate to conduct some secondary research and collect and document some narratives during my brief travels, they are documented as mere glimpses into the world across the border and are not enough to make a generalization about how Indians view Partition. I hope that one day my work allows me to explore this area further.

PART I

THE BORDER

AZAD QAIDIS

chapter one

BLURRED LINES

NASEER ASHIQ

It's 11:33 am. The date is 23 June 2012. We are driving in search of Sheikpura town, particularly Mahiwala Road, where I am supposed to conduct an interview. Corn cobs are soaking under the sun, bright yellow amongst lush green fields. Protests against electricity shortages in this Pakistani side of Punjab have delayed us. The summer sun is piercing through the windscreen, the steering wheel is hot, the mineral water bottles that we have bought from the small vendors on the way, are even hotter. We ask for directions from passersby. As they tell us to follow the road, taking an occasional left or right, I notice that the dialect has changed; the Punjabi they speak has local influences, specific to Kasur district.

Resting my elbow on the rolled-down window, I ask Iqbal Qaiser to tell me more about his uncle, whom I am to interview. His name is Muhammad Boota, he tells me. 'His home, which we are going to, is in his beloved's village. She married someone else and left for India but he continues to live there. It is as close to her as he can get.'

17

Muhammad Boota was originally from the Ballah Wallah village in Amritsar but would often come to visit his maternal grandparents in their village in Kasur, the village that we were driving in search of. It was here that he first encountered a young Sikh girl, who was later to shape the course of his life. At once attracted to her, Boota's fondness soon blossomed into intense expressions of love, and as a result his visits to his maternal village become more and more frequent.

When Partition was announced, Boota's family, like millions of others, decided to migrate to Pakistan to avoid the ensuing violence. Boota was happy; he thought the move meant he would come closer to his beloved, but 1947 had something else planned for him. The girl's family, also afraid of the news of massacres and bloodshed, thought it best to quickly marry off their daughter and together, move to the safer Indian terrority.

Iqbal sahib tells me that Boota was heartbroken but refused to let the divide separate him from his lover or the village he had grown up in at Amritsar. He says that even today, a part of his uncle's heart belongs to India. 'Until Ayub Khan took over government, my uncle used to cross the border and visit his home, which was right across, close to where he lives now. No visa was required at that time and it was very easy to trespass the boundary. Upon each illegal visit until 1965, my uncle searched for his lover. But she was nowhere to be found; no one ever saw her after Partition. My uncle, on the other hand, is still deeply in love with her. He refused to marry or even leave the village even though most members of his family are dead or have moved away.' I am excited to hear Muhammad Boota's love story and even more excited to visit a border village. I have read numerous stories in newspapers of people accidentally crossing over the border and ending up being persecuted for years. I have only been to the Wagah border so this is something new for me.

The roads become narrower and start to wind as we enter Sheikpura. It is a quiet town, with only an occasional truck or cycle passing us by. We stop the car next to a group of women sitting on a *charpai* under a mango tree. They are wearing half sleeves, with only half of their heads covered with their *dupattas*. A naked child rests in the middle, kicking his legs halfway in the air. Iqbal sahib asks them for directions to Mahiwala Road but they respond with a shy giggle, hiding their faces with the corners of their *dupattas*; they are not used to talking to strange men. We drive down a little further until we come across five or six elderly men sitting on a *charpai,* smoking from a rusty grey hookah. Next to them a young boy is getting his hair cut from the barber. They tell us to take a left and go straight.

We park the car just outside the village and make our way inwards. Mud houses surround us on both sides. It is a sleepy village, with children and buffaloes resting under tree shades; humans and nature in harmony, a site not common in urban areas. The only sounds one can hear are those of birds or the faint voices that float in from the different corners of the village. Iqbal sahib has never visited his uncle's home before. He tells me that it is his uncle who visits him in the city every few months. This is more convenient for the two as the village setting means even worse electricity shortages than in the city and poorer roads to travel on. We are told that cellphones don't work in this area; signals are cut off due to the close proximity to the border. Thus, we are testing our luck to see whether we can find his home and of course, if he is at home at all.

However, a moment later I realize that everyone seems to

know everyone here. A lady draped in a red *dupatta* points us in the direction of Muhammad Boota's house. Seconds afterwards, a man wearing an off-white *shalwar kameez* and a turban covering his head, breaks the peace of the village and asks loudly in Punjabi, 'Who are you? Please introduce yourselves.' Foreigners cannot go unidentified in this village. Iqbal sahib tells him that he is Muhammad Boota's nephew and is here to see him. The man responds abruptly, 'He isn't home. He's been gone for four-five days and we don't know when he'll return.'

Disappointed, my fiancé Haroon and I ask Iqbal sahib if we can at least see the border before returning. We had woken up in the early hours to make this trip; sightseeing was the least we could get out of it. But as we begin to move towards the line, the man in the off-white *shalwar kameez* follows us, asking what we are up to. We tell him that we just want to see the border but he continues to shadow us. Iqbal sahib seems to be in a rush as well. He quickly points towards a faraway line and says, 'That's all it is. Let's go back now.' Later he tells us that he thought that the man was from Pakistan's Inter-Services Intelligence (ISI), many of whose men roam around in civilian clothes near the border areas. Perhaps he was afraid we were Indian spies, or perhaps innocent but too-curious-for-our-own-good Pakistanis. Neither group is acceptable lurking so close to the border. This is just another symptom of the mistrust that breeds between India and Pakistan; spying seen as a necessity to ward off the suspicious 'other'. As we head back towards the car, with unfinished work, a woman and a man raise their heads from behind one of the mud houses and say, 'We overheard that you're Muhammad Boota's guests. He is like family to us. Please come inside.'

The man in the off-white *shalwar kameez* hesitates but after some serious contemplation slowly walks away, leaving us in the company of this family. As we enter their home, I observe that hundreds of red chillies are drying under the sun. Next to them, goats, tied to trees, are taking an afternoon nap. It's almost 12:15 pm.

A group of ten to twelve men, women and children rise from the two *charpais* laid out in the courtyard of the home. They scramble into one of the rooms, allowing us to sit. An infant is tied with his mother's *dupatta* right under the *charpai* that Haroon and I are invited to sit on. It serves as a makeshift cot for him, gently rocking back and forth each time the wind blows. Iqbal sahib sits across us with the man of the house, Naseer Ashiq (the name has been changed to protect his identity), sixty-five. His wife rushes inside and brings out three glasses of Mountain Dew which we gulp down, as a refuge from the heat. They haven't had any electricity since 7 am, she tells me as she hands us handmade fans to relieve ourselves.

Iqbal sahib explains to Ashiq that I wanted to speak with his uncle regarding his visits to India in the early years. He laughs and responds in Punjabi, 'Then you should have come here a few days later, on third *sawan* (from the local calendar). A huge *mela* (festival) is held that day where Indians and Pakistanis come together to pray at the *mazaar* (shrine), just on the zero line.' I lean forward with interest, wanting to know more about the festival that brings together two historic enemies. However, despite belonging to Lahore, a city that lies at the heart of Punjab, I have never been taught to speak Punjabi as part of the modern education system, and have only recently started to learn it on my own; it is, after all, seen as an uncultured language confined to rural corners, not suitable for the educated and 'civilized' elite. I turn towards Haroon and ask him to translate for me; he is far more fluent than I am. I want to know everything about this *mela*.

The *mela*, as we find out, has been held since before Partition and continues till date. Indians and Pakistanis both attend, under the vigilant eyes of the rangers. They bring food and *mithai*, and greet each other from across the line. First the Indian group is allowed to pray at the shrine and then the Pakistani lot.

If I am to believe Naseer Ashiq, the border, which is meant to divide on the basis of religion, serves as a source of connection for Indians and Pakistanis for religious reasons itself. Together they come to offer their prayers, in their own customary manner, at a shrine that they both revere and respect—a shrine that is Hindu, Sikh and Muslim; each to his or her own. Religious and geographical distinctions come to be blurred at the line of division itself.

This is paradoxical, almost self-contradictory, to say the least. Born in the late eighties, I have grown up hearing stories about Hindu, Muslim and Sikh divisions, about how the communities could not live together primarily because they could no longer practise their religions side by side. A new country had to be formed: Muslims were a separate nation; their practices were at extreme variance with the non-Muslims of India. 'They' worshipped multiple idols, 'we' worshipped 'one Allah'. There was nothing mutual; there were no grounds for unity. Separation was necessary. To hear that Hindus, Sikhs and Muslims could seek blessings at the same shrine, that they could come together to greet, hug and celebrate together, is an anomaly for me. To unite on top of that at the very border which is meant to divide is almost satirical. For Naseer Ashiq, however, this is the only normal that he knows. Later, I am to find out that there are many other such *melas* that take place across the country. At some of these, for instance at Baisakhi at Ram Thamman, in Kasur district, local Muslims and non-Muslims come together to celebrate, while at others, the festivals take place at the LoC or other lines of division across the country and Indians and Pakistanis come forward in celebration from both sides.

'It was here at this *mela* that my father, Saraf Din, met his Sikh family after 1947 for the first time.' Sikh family? His father was a Sikh? Taken aback, I interrupt him in English, looking at Haroon in complete confusion while Ashiq in return looks at me puzzled, unsure of what I just said in the foreign language. I ask Haroon to confirm whether Naseer Ashiq belongs to a Sikh family that continued to stay on this side of the border. That would be most fascinating for in a land of 3 per cent minorities, it is not common to run into non-Muslims. But no, he answers. 'I am a Muslim and so was my father but he was adopted by a Sikh in India before Partition. He didn't have any children so he asked my grandparents to give him my father.' I wonder how Saraf Din's parents felt about him having a Sikh upbringing, but Ashiq brushes off my question with a shrug. It holds no value for him; nor is it something that has concerned him. For Ashiq the situation is simple. 'The Sikh gentleman brought up my father with so much love and devotion that my biological grandparents were only happy and as a reward, God graced him with four sons and a daughter later on. His other sons, my *chachas* (uncles), were called Sucha Singh, Acher Singh, Bajna Singh and Khoja Singh.' He doesn't find it necessary to mention the daughter, his aunt's name. 'The Sikh family was my father's real family. Even when the Partition riots broke out and Sikhs and Muslims were killing each other, the Sikh gentleman ensured that my father was safely sent to Pakistan.'

Saraf Din was fifty-five at the time of Partition and looked just like a Sikh, wearing a *pagri* and beard matching that of his father and brothers. To me this sounds almost surreal; a Muslim boy with a Sikh father and Sikh brothers and sisters. However, I am told that contrary to what most Pakistanis and Indians like myself believe today, such hazy divisions were common in the pre-Partition days, when communities intermingled with each other, their identities getting diluted in the process. Ashiq, unlike myself, has grown up hearing such stories from his father. His understanding of the 'other' is not rigid like mine, nor is the division between India and Pakistan and Indians and Pakistanis as stark. Living at the border, where he can see Indians across from him, further reiterates the arbitrariness of the lines of division. Despite the armed forces and border controls, he has probably come into contact with far more Indians than the ordinary Pakistani. They are not strange and imaginary figures for him but instead, are a part of his daily existence.

He tells me that long into the nights, Saraf Din would cry, yearning for his family even several years after Partition. It was only fifty-seven years ago at the border *mela* that he was able to momentarily meet with them. Sitting at the border line in Pakistan, he yelled across at familiar faces. Instantly recognizing each other, they tightly embraced, tears streaming down their faces. At that time Ashiq was a young child, more interested in the *mela*, its lights, sounds, sweets and people, than the strange men his father was so jubilant to meet.

However, today he longs to meet them. He tells me it would be a way to remember his father, a way to connect with him after his death. But he has not been successful; he has returned empty-handed from the Indian High Commission in Islamabad three times over the past few years. 'We have given up.' His shoulders droop as he says this, his body language a testimony to the words coming out of his mouth. '*Bara dil karta hai jane ka, bohat mohabbat hai Hindustan se*' (I really want to visit India, I feel a lot of love for the country and its people), he adds in Urdu for me, his eyes moist. 'We have tried to keep in touch with the family. They once wrote a letter to us but no one here understands Gurmukhi, and there they don't understand Punjabi or Urdu scripts. I even went to the city to get my reply translated into Gurmukhi but they never wrote back. Maybe they don't live at that address anymore. I sometimes wonder if I'll ever speak to them again.'

A few years ago at the *mela* he tried to spot the family. The rangers told him that if he could recognize them, they would allow them to meet. However, it had been years since he saw them so he sat across, unable to identify his uncles in the midst of the strangers. I ask him how he feels about the lines of separation that divided his father and now him from his paternal family.

'Those were different times altogether that my father lived through. It is painful, this imposed division. But I cannot say I am as sad about it as my father was. Yes, by meeting his family I would be able to fulfil his dying wish, I could serve him as his son, even if in his death . . . but my association with India isn't as strong. I was only a few months old at Partition. I was brought up here, here in Pakistan. For me, what was sadder was when our *pind* was taken away from us during the 1971 war.'

Similar to Ashiq, I had once met a man in Multan who had travelled all the way from India to find his mother's ancestral home. He told me that his mother had died crying for the home she had left behind in Pakistan at Partition. When she died, he decided to fulfil her wish on her behalf. Here in Pakistan he had come to locate her house and take a piece of it back in the form of a brick to be buried next to her. For him and Ashiq, the 'other' side perhaps did not hold much personal significance. The 'other' was understood through their parents, and in this case through their love and losses. The children wanted to give their parents peace in the afterlife which they were unable to achieve during their lifetime. But beyond that, they had their own lives, their own struggles.

When war broke out in 1971 for the separation of East Pakistan, bombs would be dropped on Naseer Ashiq's village. Scared residents ran away to nearby places, like Kasur city, Ram Thamman or Khurpa Chak in Raiwind. The Indian police took over the area and Ashiq had to knock door-to-door for about eleven to twelve months before his village was returned to its people, after the Simla Agreement was signed between India and Pakistan. When they returned, they saw that three or four elders of the community, who were too old to flee, were nowhere to be found. Baba Mahi and Baba Gulu were amongst them. 'I don't know whether the Indians took them or what happened . . .'

Naseer Ashiq had a similar experience during the 1965 Indo-Pak war, although the situation was reversed for him at that time. The Pakistan Army took over Indian property and a number of Indian villages, including Ashiq's mother's ancestral home, became a part of Pakistan overnight. For months, Ashiq would walk around the area, drinking water from his mother's ancestral village and resting at other Indian hamlets. He tells us that just as the Indians had looted his village during the 1971 war, the Muslims looted these villages. The irony is that many times both sides ended up stealing from their own ancestral lands.

Naseer Ashiq offers to walk us to the border, barely half a kilometre away. His village is the closest village to the line of division. While 1947 preceded his conscious years and thereby failed to directly impact him, his home and its geography continue to ensure that the repercussions of Partition do not evade him. He lives in a place which is a constant reminder of historical events, where home can overnight be taken and given at the whim of political and military movements. He is to lurk in between, the instability caused by Partition affecting him even six decades later. As we walk through the fields, burning sand covers my sandals. Alongside, young children bathe in the canal to beat the heat of June. Some wave at us, amused by this alien intrusion on a Saturday afternoon.

Leading the way, Ashiq casually lifts his hand and says, 'Look there. That row of plants divides the Indian land from the Pakistani. Next to it you can see a milestone. If you cross that, the Indian rangers would come and ask you to go back.' It is in this moment, as we stand here armed on both sides, that I realize that we are only inches away from India. Embankments surround us, army tanks visible from a distance. The last time I was at the border, my experience was very different. Back in February 2012, I had crossed the Wagah border on foot. As my companions rushed excitedly to the other side, I had taken a moment to stand in the middle of the no-man's-land—land belonging neither to India nor Pakistan. On one side, the Pakistani crescent and star, alongside the *kalma* and Quaid-e-Azam Muhammad Ali Jinnah's picture, stared back at me; on the other end, a portrait of Mahatma Gandhi amongst the orange, white and green of the Indian flag welcomed me to India. The crossing over had been decisive, the entry and exit points of the two countries clearly defined. Sikh officials, wearing colourful turbans, were waiting on one side. Pakistani men dressed in uniform stared from a distance.

Standing here at the border in Kasur, where the only visible lines of division are a distant wire or plants that would usually be found growing in people's homes, distorts the fine separation. One step backward and we are safe, one step forward and we will have to face serious repercussions, landing up in another country, and that too an 'enemy state'.

'People often cross over accidentally. Once we had guests over for a wedding. Right after eating food, they rushed over to see the border and walked too far. We had to pull many strings to get them back,' Ashiq laughs. This is routine business for them. 'We work here every day. The Indians over there, and us here. The rangers watch us closely, ensuring that we don't talk. But we are allowed to look at each other. You know, their women never come to the fields like ours do. The men bring their own food in the morning.'

According to Naseer Ashiq, even until 1986 there was no line or wire demarcating the border as it does today. People could easily sneak in. Iqbal sahib's uncle, who I had originally come to meet, was one of them. Today rangers are stricter, only allowing the farmers to work within a certain time frame. They have to record their entry and exit and the officials follow them much more closely.

From where we stand, we can see both Indian and Pakistani check posts. Men and women are busy planting rice on the Pakistani side. Far away, one can see Indian workers sowing seeds under the blazing sun that they both share. 'Often some of our animals cross over but the Indian officials give them back to us without any trouble,' Ashiq finishes off as he leads us back to his home.

It's about 1:30 pm by the time we leave the area. Ashiq has invited us all to the *mela* which will take place next month. Exhausted by spending mere minutes in the field, we stop for more water on our way out. Seeing my excitement about what we had just experienced, Iqbal sahib tells me of another man who lives in a border village, called Padhana. This village is situated right across an Indian village, Nowshera. When Partition happened, the man's village was shaken by violent protests against Muslims. With only the clothes on his back he ran out of Indian Nowshera. After a few kilometres, he reached Padhana, which was now part of the newly-formed state of Pakistan, meant to be a safe haven for Muslims like him. From where he continues to live, his home is within the reach of sight. Every morning, he wakes up to see his ancestral village, his *pind*, his people and the places that have been part of his existence since birth. 'Guru Har Gobind's gurdwara is right across too. If you look closely, you can see it,' he told Iqbal sahib. However, despite being just kilometres away from his home, he is unable to visit his people or walk across to them. Under the laws of both countries, the residents of these border villages are not allowed to talk to each other either. They can work freely within their perimeters, exchanging glances, experiencing the same weather and work conditions, but are unable to communicate through the common language which they both speak, despite being a few metres away. Iqbal sahib laughs at the irony, 'These are our *azad qaidis* (free prisoners),' he says, and I smile at how aptly he puts it; these are truly the prisoners of Partition, caught right in between two hostile states.

As we drive towards Kasur city, our conversation reminds me of another *azad qaidi*, a hostage of the Partition aftermath. Sitting imprisoned in a bus that was to transport him from Wagah to Batala, Muhammad Rauf had related to me how he had looked out at his city, his birth place, his home: Amritsar. That was the closest he was going to get to it.

chapter two

THE BUS THAT DID NOT STOP

MUHAMMAD RAUF

'Daughter, if you were kicked out of your home for fifty or sixty years and then you returned but were unable to see it, how would you feel? When I saw Putlighar, I began to cry. I had grown up there, I had lived there but I couldn't get out for a minute and roam around. The bus couldn't stop and even if it had, I couldn't have stepped out . . .'

This was the first time after 1947 that Muhammad Rauf (the name has been changed to protect his identity), now seventy-four, saw the city he was born and raised in, one that he had left behind at the tender age of nine. The well that he drank water from as a child, the grounds where he played flashed across behind the tinted windows of the bus. Leaning closer towards the windscreen to make out the moving images, Rauf had tried to spot his school, to see the lanes where he had grown up. But the glass stood in the middle, the buildings and alleys becoming a blur as the bus sped on its way.

Rauf had migrated to Pakistan a few months prior to

31

Partition. Though his memory was foggy and he didn't remember exact dates when I spoke with him, he told me that it was around June 1947 and he was studying in second grade at a primary school in Putlighar, where he was born and brought up, when riots ripped through his hometown. Frightened and confused by what was transpiring outside, his family decided to scramble to Lahore for a few weeks. Taking none of their belongings along, certain to return as soon as things settled down, their world changed when Partition was announced. 'We had locked our house from the outside. We thought it was a matter of a few days before things normalized. I didn't know I'd never see my home again. None of us knew that Partition was going to happen, we didn't even know what it meant for us.' Sixty-two years later, he had returned to his city but due to the strict policies between India and Pakistan, Rauf could not see Amritsar; he did not have the visa to go 'home'.

Unlike any other country I have visited, India and Pakistan only issue city visas, and that too for a maximum of five cities at a time; this in itself is a recent achievement. As a result, visitors are only able to visit the cities they hold visas for, no detouring or additional stops are allowed. In case one trespasses this law, serious legal repercussions may have to be faced. In Rauf's case, he had only managed to get a visa for Qadian, his main destination, and Batala, where he was going to stop in transit. As an Ahmadi, a sect that has been declared non-Muslim in Pakistan since the 1970s, Rauf crossed the border to be a part of the Qadiani *Jalsa* (procession) taking place in Qadian, where Mirza Ghulam Muhammad, the founder of the Ahmadiyya community, was born. To get visas for other cities may have been possible in theory but getting separate invitation letters from different cities is a struggle; the invitee needs to be credible, a No Objection Certificate needs to be obtained, stamps of the first magistrate in each city are required. For the majority of people, especially those who do not have many contacts across the border, finding such invitees can be an arduous task. For Rauf, this meant that his birthplace, Amritsar, was not going to be on the agenda on this visit.

As I sat with him on a hot summer afternoon, I had asked Rauf about what had happened at Partition, as a result of which he had to leave Amritsar permanently. I was glad that he spoke a mix of Urdu and Punjabi, making it easier for me to converse with him without constantly looking sideways for help. With some difficulty and a few awkward beginnings, he was able to revisit some of the painful memories of that fateful year. 'My family sought shelter amongst hundreds of other refugees at the Walton Camp in Lahore. We stayed there for over a week before my cousin, who was enrolled in the army, was able to safely transport us in an army convoy to Sahiwal, a city about two hours away from Lahore.' He had started speaking with a shiver, the memories alight in him. 'There were so many people at the camp, cramped in the tents with us. Young, old, children, women; all of us trying to make it through the day . . .'

Partition happened in the humid month of August, which also happened to be the holy month of fasting for Muslims. With the thousands of migrants pouring in from across the border, the Pakistani government was given the enormous task of housing them, with minimum resources and a lack of expertise. The world hadn't seen such massive migration—it is estimated that about 15 million people lost their homes in

1947.[4] There was no precedent. 'We would get *daal* and *roti* (lentils and bread) once a day. This was a luxury. With so many people homeless, we were grateful for whatever little we could get.' The makeshift tents at the largest camp in Lahore were home to Rauf's family; they lived there amongst corpses, the diseased and the injured for days. 'If someone died, their families would hide them, afraid that the authorities would start rationing less food to them.

'We got off at Sahiwal because it seemed safe but when we got to the refugee camp at Mall Mandi, the conditions were horrible. There were hundreds of people scattered everywhere with no place to walk, no bathroom, nothing. We lived here for a few months before we were given evacuee property.' Sahiwal, known as Montegomery under the British era, is a small city. Known for the largest railway platform in Pakistan and a central jail that has housed notable personalities from Nehru and Zulfikar Ali Bhutto to Faiz and Habib Jalib, today Sahiwal is a peaceful town.

I had driven there with my colleagues to conduct oral history interviews of the Partition generation for the Citizens Archive of Pakistan (CAP), the organization that I worked for. We had already conducted four interviews by the time we met with Muhammad Rauf. The electricity had been gone for the past ten hours. It was about 4 pm and the UPS had given up too. Enclosed in a small room to ensure good audio quality, we fanned ourselves with the newspapers and magazines lying nearby.

Rauf had become very quiet as he reflected on the Partition

---

[4] 1947 Archive, *About Partition*, Web: http://www.1947partitionarchive.org/?q=press_release

days, and for a while none us had spoken, but when he did, he had gone back to his childhood in Amritsar. 'Opposite my school in Putlighar was a Christian graveyard and in front of my house, there was a railway crossing,' he had begun. 'The street I used to live on was called the 'cool street' because there were so many large trees planted on both sides. It was so popular in the summer that you had people coming there for their evening walks. There was even this huge well besides it and the water there used to get so cold that one couldn't drink it all at once . . .' His eyes were misty as he recalled his early days but there was a jovial undercurrent in his voice. These were memories that he was happy to share. This was before all the tension had started, before he had been separated from his home. 'All of us naughty children from the community would collect around the well after school. When we would see Sikh boys coming home, we would snatch their notebooks,' he had chuckled, 'but it was all in good fun, we were great friends. We spent some wonderful times together, playing sports, teasing our teachers . . . and then on every Eid and Lohri, we would always come together and celebrate. *Woh josh hi kuch aur tha* (that spirit was something different altogether). We would wear clean clothes and take them some sweets and they would do the same for us. We had great relations . . . a lot of love between us.' In the evenings, Rauf would play with the other children in the community, which included Muslims, Hindus and Sikhs. 'We would play *luggun mithi*. Do you know what that is? It's what you call *chuppan chupai* (hide and seek) these days. We would play until 9 or 10 in the night, with not a care in the world. *Woh bus keh lo ke azadi thi* (you can say that was the real freedom).

'When I went to India for the religious procession, I got to see a little bit of Amritsar again. You know, it is as wonderful as it used to be, the people even lovelier.'

I had wanted to know more about this crossing over and had asked him to tell me everything. The idea for this book had not come to the forefront at this time but there was something in his voice that pushed me to diverge from Partition and ask him about his journey to his birthplace. Belonging to a migrant family from Batala myself, one who had never returned to her roots after Partition, I knew this wasn't an opportunity that everyone got. But Rauf told me that his fond memories were also limited to the border itself.

Prepared that he would have to board the bus to his destination as soon as he was cleared at the immigration point at Wagah, it did not even cross Rauf's mind that standing at the border was the closest he had been to Putlighar in the last six decades. 'It was the first time I was leaving the country and I was scared about how they would treat me at the border. I just wanted to get the paperwork out of the way and get to Qadian.' It was almost as if he had pushed his pre-Partition life to the back of his mind, not registering that he was inches away from his birth place. But Rauf was in for a surprise. As he was going to find out, he had nothing to worry about; 'they' were only going to facilitate him in every way imaginable.

As Rauf handed his passport to a Sikh official behind the counter, anxious to see his response to a Pakistani passport, he saw the officer's expression change into one of excitement. Confused, Rauf turned around to see what the official was smiling about, but all he saw were more Pakistani men and women waiting in the line to get their passports stamped. Rauf was still standing there apprehensively when the official exclaimed, '*Oye dekh, ye saada apna hai!*' (Oh look! He's one of our own.) Baffled, Rauf told himself that he must have heard wrong and proceeded to the next counter. But here too upon seeing his passport the officer yelled out, '*Oye Pathoo, oye dekh saada banda hai. Changi taran dekhi, koi kisi kism ki gal baat na hoey.*' (He's one of us. Make sure you take good care of him, no one should bother him.) The officer told Rauf to take a seat while he completed all his paperwork for him. No strings had been pulled, no side payments had been made. The service he had been provided with was entirely at the whim of the officer.

I was just as perplexed hearing about this as Rauf had been at that moment. Harassment at the Indo-Pak border is fairly common. Intelligence officials, in and out of uniform, patrol the area, suspicious of the tourists and their agendas. This kind of reaction is not found at the line of division. Worried why he was being associated with the Sikhs, Muhammad Rauf asked himself, '*Mein inka kaise ho gaya?*' (How am I one of them?) It was only once his immigration was complete that he realized the reason for this: his passport said, 'Born in Amritsar.'

His voice had broken down as he narrated this story to us. 'I was still one of them . . . even after all these years,' he said softly. 'It made me realize that I was at my birthplace, my home town, and all of a sudden I had this desperate urge to see it. The way I had been greeted by the Sikhs had brought back memories of my childhood spent with them. It made me want to go see my house, my school, to meet my friends . . .' Memories Rauf had learnt to sideline over the decades had come rushing back and there was an aching desire to reconnect. But unfortunately, laws and legalities stood in the way. With his head lowered, he told us, 'I smelled the air of my land, I stood under its open sky, but within seconds we were shoved into a bus. Our time in Amritsar was over.'

For a moment no one spoke. The only sound in the room was that of the newspapers swaying back and forth in our hands. But after a few seconds he had looked up, as if after great speculation and with some guilt, and confessed, 'I felt so desperate in that moment that I bribed the bus driver to take a detour and show us Amritsar . . . for just a few minutes . . . I couldn't return without seeing any of it . . . this was my home.' At first he was wary of how we would react and felt the need to justify his actions—to travel in India or Pakistan without the required permit could only mean trouble; just the previous day two Indians had been arrested in Pakistan for illegally entering Mirpur when their visa was only valid for Rawalpindi. Rauf knew what he had done could be considered a criminal offence. But when he saw that we were too engrossed in his story to care about what was right or wrong, he decided to continue. 'The driver was a good man. He obliged me, half because of the money I offered and half because he understood my pain, he thought of me as his own, just like the officials had.' The bus driver took Rauf and his companions, other Ahmadis from Pakistan, for a quick ride around the city. 'We saw the Company Bagh, the Golden Temple and even Putlighar!' Any shame he had felt in disclosing this information was replaced with renewed energy; his eyes were alive, his face lit up as he reminisced about these places. Sitting on the edge of his seat, Rauf had seen that Putlighar had developed over the years but the well he drank from as a student, the signboards in Gurmukhi, and the colourful Sikh *pagris* were amongst the many things he could relate to. After all, they formed some of the earliest memories of his childhood.

Within minutes, however, the driver had gone back on track, puffing away from Putlighar and on to Batala, and then

Qadian. 'We were getting late and many of the passengers were impatient ... they didn't have any interest in what I wanted to see ... to them they were just old streets that we were driving through aimlessly.'

During our conversation, Rauf had briefly mentioned that the rest of his stay in India had been quite pleasant. The Indians had been wonderful to his group, especially upon hearing they were from Pakistan. Attending the *jalsa* also held great spiritual value for Rauf. This *jalsa* dates back 112 years and is of prime importance to the Ahmadiyya community. But in Rauf's own words, 'Nothing beat that feeling at the border, at Amritsar, to be amongst my people and my land, even for mere minutes.'

I found it strange that until his visit to the border, Rauf had almost forgotten his past in Amritsar, that he hadn't even tried getting a multiple-city visa. Was it only the Sikhs at the border that had pushed him to remember? Was it so easy to forget? Or was that the only strategy the Partition survivors could employ in face of the loss and displacement that was thrust upon them?

Before I could ask him any of this, his wife walked in with bubbling glasses of Sprite. Looking sideways at her husband, she told us that he was unwell and shouldn't be speaking for so long. We had apologized for taking so much time and quickly started to pack up. It was time to go back to Lahore. These questions would have to wait for later. As I bent forward so that Rauf could run his hands over my head, blessing me with a long life, I realized that droplets had lined his eyes. Speaking about Amritsar had made him nostalgic. The thought of not being able to see it again had brought about grief, an aching realization of the loss, of being so close to his home yet being so restricted, caged away in a twenty-seater. Pressing his hand gently over my head, he had said, 'Woh Amritsar si, Rauf di paidaiesh si. Jo jagah meri paidaiesh hai, mein kisi se gul baat na kar saka. Raat na reh saka. Woh shehar tou mera hai magar itni ijazat nahi si ke mein kisi se utar ke mil loon. Oh border hi si jahan kisi ne merey naal dhang se baat ki.' (Amritsar was my birthplace but I couldn't talk to anyone there, I couldn't spend a night there. That city was mine but I didn't even have the permission to get out and meet my friends and neighbours. It was only at the border that I was spoken to properly.)

This pain is echoed by millions who lost and can no longer claim what was rightfully theirs, who cannot go back to meet loved ones, to see their homes one last time. This pain, as I was to find out, was going to resonate in many of the interviews I was going to conduct after that day.

As we drove to Kasur city for lunch at what Iqbal sahib called the local Pearl Continental Hotel (a five-star hotel in Lahore), I wondered how many more stories there were out there. Stories of people living inches away from their home but being unable to speak, to see, to hear and to touch what was once their own. The migrant in Padhana stared at his home from right across the border, Naseer Ashiq (Chapter One) and his father sat at the line of division in search of their family, and Muhammad Rauf came closest to his home from within a bus, looking out at his heritage from behind a two-by-two window.

Two years later, when I travelled to what is referred to as Azad Kashmir in Pakistan and Pakistan-occupied Kashmir in India, I came across a multitude of such stories. There, the Neelum River, or Kishanganga as it is known in India, served as an arbitrary border. Each wave symbolized a division between this side and that. Our guesthouse was situated on the bank of the river, our view was India, our bedroom was in Pakistan. It was the most surreal experience I had ever been through. Across from my room was a mosque. It was located in Indian Kashmir but served as a call for prayer for both Pakistani and Indian Muslims. There were daughters on one side and mothers on the other. I was told that here families are allowed to talk to one another and thus, when the river quietens after the monsoon months, families sit across from each other by the riverside and converse in the only way they know. For these families, the watery lines form a part of their identity. The LoC is an everyday reality for them, it divides them and yet it is often only at this LoC that they can reunite, where they can sit in front of each other and discuss their daily lives.

The border, on one hand, acts as an explicit denial of unity; a constant reminder to stay away. There is no room to err at the India-Pakistan border. The consequences are life-altering, as witnessed by the thousands that languish in Pakistani and Indian jails; their crime only crossing over accidentally. And yet, for many of the people I had spoken to, the border also symbolized the only connection with the other. It was the border which brought these people close to their relatives, to their homes and their people, for however short a time and in whatever limited manner. Sucha Singh, Bajna Singh, Acher Singh and Khoja Singh could only embrace their brother at the line of division. Padhana's migrant could only see his home in Nowshera standing at the border. Rauf only set foot in his city at Wagah—he could only inhale the air of his land standing at the foot of the border. The line which was meant to create distance was the only point where they could connect.

Yes, trespassing any further was dangerous. But standing here, it was acceptable to look; for a few minutes it was possible to become a part of one's past, a part of one's family. Visas and stamped papers stood in the way of anything else. This was the only relief these families were going to get. The *mela,* the riverside conversations, the permission to look across and absorb what was intrinsically theirs sustained the bonds that these people had on the other side. The border that had caused the separation was apologetic; reuniting them for a fleeting moment was its act of penance.

PART II

FAMILIES PARTITIONED

WHEN HOME IS ELSEWHERE

chapter three

TEA AT NO-MAN'S-LAND

TINA VACHANI

'I was standing right across from him. I could see my father wave at me while he pleaded with the Pakistani officials to talk to the Indians, to let me come just a little forward. But they wouldn't allow it. That was the last time I saw him, from behind the Indian gate at Wagah.'

At the age of fourteen, Tina was torn apart from her parents. She was a Pakistani by birth, an Indian by her roots. Born in Karachi, she and her siblings were brought up by her parents. Tina's paternal family belonged to Jalandhar and maternal family had settled in Delhi at Partition. But it was not enough to have her history and heritage scattered between the two lands. Soon after she touched her teens, she was to leave behind her family and home in Karachi for the unfamiliarity of Delhi. Unknowingly, her life was to become a jigsaw puzzle, pieces and patches of laughter, memories and pain stitched together to make her the woman she is today. As the brainchild and founder of Routes2Roots (R2R), a Delhi-based cultural, non-profit organization dedicated to encouraging dialogue, interaction and cultural exchange among SAARC countries, specially between India and Pakistan, Tina's work has the baggage of her past and the grief of separation entrenched in it. I speak to her one morning while she is seated at her office in New Delhi.

'It had been years since I had seen my family ... I was desperate to catch a glimpse of them, to hug my mother and father, to sit with them for just a little while. We had tried for six or seven years to get a visa, for them to come to India or me to go to Pakistan, but nothing had worked out. Meeting at the border was our last resort.'

Tina's father, Jagdish Anand, had moved alone as a young man from Jalandhar to what later became Pakistan. Fascinated with the film industry, he had set up Eveready Pictures in Karachi in 1946, with the intention of flying in and out of Mumbai and connecting with the film fraternity there at his will. When Partition took place, he didn't feel that there would be any major change in his lifestyle. Despite belonging to a Hindu family, he felt no need to move. His business, his wife, his friends and entire life was embedded on that side of the border. India would remain within reach, crisscrossing ever so easy. And in the first few years, this proved to be true. Tina tells me she would come to visit her grandparents and cousins, most of whom were settled in Delhi, during every school vacation. Travelling was far easier at this time, passengers only requiring a permit to cross over. In any case, Jagdish had many contacts in the film industry; he could pull strings other Pakistanis and Indians could not.

Tina's relatives would welcome her with open arms, excited not only to meet family but also to hear stories about Karachi and receive the foreign goodies she would bring with her. As

India had adopted a closed economy model in line with the Soviet model of development, imports were restricted at the time. Foreign goods had thus become a luxury. Meanwhile, in Pakistan, such goods were aplenty. In fact, on the whole, Tina tells me that Karachi was far more affluent and developed as compared to the Delhi of that time.

'I would be treated as a special guest, the kind from overseas ... America or England. The modern facilities we had in Pakistan at this time weren't available in India so in a way I felt looked up to by my cousins.' I express my surprise. The Pakistan I have grown up in has more than often been stereotyped as backward, un-modern, dirty and poor. India, in comparison, has been the rising elephant, if not the tiger; the neighbour that stands tall, aggressively shouldering a much smaller and less developed nation to its west. Seeing my reaction, Tina laughs, 'You have no idea how wonderful and vibrant Karachi was back then. It was a happening and buzzing place. I was studying at St. Jospeh Convent School and I had made so many friends ... some of the closest ones that I remember were Sabrina, Rubina, Lubna ... I never missed not having our relatives or cousins in Pakistan. Karachiites were known to be friendly and so even our neighbours on Tariq Road—who by the way included the famous actor Waheed Murad—had become more like family.

'Karachi was so cosmopolitan, with people from so many different communities. There were many other non-Muslims, Gujaratis, Sindhis ... we would celebrate Diwali and all other Hindu festivals and my Muslim friends would come ... they would be excited ... they would light fireworks and *diyas* with me. It was a very common thing ... I never even thought much about being a minority. We've seen those days.'

Karachi, even today, is referred to as one of the most cosmopolitan and multicultural cities in Pakistan. Unlike Punjab, which is far more homogenous in its identity, Sindh remains host to multiple ethnicities, religions and castes. I can imagine that this was even more so in the early years of Pakistan.

Tina had come to Delhi right before the 1971 war broke out, which led to the separation of East Pakistan and the creation of Bangladesh. 'I had come to visit my grandparents after giving my 10th grade examinations when the war was announced. Instantly, all communication channels were snapped off; I was stuck here in India and my parents there in Pakistan and we couldn't even talk to each other. It was a terrible state. I didn't know what was going to happen. The last thing one wants is to be a victim of war, to be uprooted from family and trapped away from home. Imagine not being able to go back home for seven or eight years. I just could not go back . . .'

'By the time my parents and I tried to meet at the border I was already in my early twenties . . . so much had changed . . . so many things had happened in my life. My father told me that he and my mother would come from the Lahore side and I should travel to Amritsar from Delhi to meet them. He had used his contacts and said we could probably sit and have tea at no-man's-land. I was so excited . . . I had so much to tell them, so much to ask . . . about home, about our neighbours, my friends . . .'

I cannot imagine the situation, the grief of being yanked away from family. I remember once when I was studying in Canada and the news about bomb blasts and insecurity in Pakistan was being broadcast on all the television channels there. I was meant to return home for summer vacations and complete an internship at the Human Rights Commission of Pakistan. However, the administration at McGill University, where I was studying, was afraid to let me go. 'It's unsafe; we highly recommend you don't leave. We won't bear any responsibility.' I recall feeling frustrated; how could they stop me from going home, whatever conditions it may be in? Later, my mother had to sign a letter that I would be living at home with her and if anything went wrong, the university would not be held accountable. That was the closest I had been to being forced to stay away from home. I could thus certainly not imagine what Tina had asked me to.

I ask her why she couldn't return, why she didn't go back after the war ended, when the situation normalized between the two countries. In a couple of articles and interviews I had read about Tina in the Indian media, I had come across different stories. Some said her parents had sent her to India before the war deliberately, to avoid the unstable conditions in Pakistan; others said she came here to avoid the poor education system in Pakistan. Yet others stated that she had come to India to get married; that there was no good Hindu *rishta* at home. The days of her arrival were also all over the place, some citing it before the war and others after. When I speak to Tina, I can understand where some of this confusion arises from. As a young fourteen-year-old, those initial years in India formed the most difficult time of her life. When I ask her questions about that period, she becomes confused, uncertain, almost as if she is a young child again. 'I was like a lost person in this entire ocean of the unknown,' she says in a frail voice, and I notice that her earlier bubbly tone is gone.

She tells me she doesn't remember the exact dates, the exact complications or what one may call the facts of that time. That wasn't what was important to her. It was how her life was unfolding in between those events that forever changed her. She tells me she had come to India for an ordinary visit, to meet her grandparents as she did every year. But after the war she had to give up her Pakistani nationality, she had to apply for the naturalization process to become an Indian, which took approximately seven to eight years and during which time she was not allowed to leave the country. She doesn't clarify why she had to give up her Pakistani passport; she makes it sound like a bureaucratic hurdle, a result of the war.

Perhaps this is true, perhaps it was just a case of red tape and idiotic laws. Or perhaps, her family had felt this was the best decision for her at that time. I cannot be certain for Tina doesn't answer my questions. She tells me nothing made sense to her. After all, why would being torn away from family, friends and one's home make sense? She says she doesn't want to go down memory lane, that it is too tragic. All she remembers is what renouncing her Pakistani nationality meant; it meant that she could not travel home for many years. That for those years, she would no longer be a Pakistani nor an Indian, that she would belong nowhere. She seems rushed and reluctant and I realize I shouldn't probe further, that it was dangerous to push someone into the traumatic years that they wanted to forget; that I had to be sensitive as a researcher. But the questions that had arisen in my mind could not be quieted, even if I could only address them to myself.

Supposing that her renouncing her Pakistani nationality and becoming an Indian was a choice her family had made at that time, even before the war; that they had wanted her to have the best of the two worlds, I wonder if they knew the consequences of such a decision. The conflict between East and West Pakistan had been escalating for a while but they could not have foreseen the extent of the war, of the divide between the two sides, which only worsened in the years to come. Imagine the overbearing feeling of responsibility; of assuming you are making the ideal choice for your daughter, that she would easily be able to come and go, to only realize that was the last time you would see her? That you had torn her apart from her family at such a young age, that she could not return even for a visit for years? Whether Tina's stay in India was a bureaucratic hurdle, a result of the war, or a well-thought-out plan by her family, I have no doubt that both she and her family felt the repercussions day in and day out, in India and Pakistan.

'The maternal side of my family, which was based in Delhi, helped me apply for citizenship and my passport. Since I was in India I had to start my education over there too. War had just gotten over a year or so ago and people still had their biases. It wasn't easy to be accepted. There were so many questions people had about me, about Pakistan. Some would ask all of them while others wouldn't talk to me at all. Even when I went to university, it was really hard. The acceptance wasn't as easy as it would have been for a girl from Delhi or anywhere else in India. Often students would ask, '*Tum burqa pehenti thi?*' (You used to wear a *burqa?*) And I would feel so angry. How could they be so ignorant? But then I couldn't blame them, people had this generalized concept of Pakistan by then that it was backward and that the people there were narrow-minded.'

I want to know whether Tina's own family also held such opinions. How did they treat her? I wonder aloud. I remember Hina Akhtar (the name has been changed to protect her identity)—or Rupa Mehra (the name has been changed to protect her identity)—who I had once come across in Lahore. Belonging to a Hindu family that never migrated to India, Rupa converted to Islam later to marry her Pakistani Muslim husband. But till today, Rupa has not been accepted in India or Pakistan. She is a former Hindu and thus she can never be a true Pakistani. And, of course, she can't be an Indian either; she is disloyal for not migrating to India at Partition and for marrying a Pakistani Muslim and then converting to his religion. She is of neither land; no one wants to claim her. Thankfully, Tina's experience was different. 'I lived with my *nana-nani* (maternal grandparents) till I got married. They were delighted to have me with them. But it was still a huge thing for me. When you're visiting a place for a holiday your mindset is different but when you know you're there to stay for good, then the comparisons between people, home and family come forth. The warmth of the family was always there, which was great, but you have to go through each day, building your own life around you.'

It was only in 1977, when Tina had grown into a young woman, that she next saw a glimpse of her parents. Just as she had desperately tried to visit them, they had tried many times to come to India. However, visa troubles after the war and her father's heart condition had prevented them from meeting. 'I remember travelling with my *mamu jaan* (maternal uncle) to Amritsar and then to Wagah. From the other side, my father and mother had travelled from Karachi to Lahore. They were accompanied by their dear friends from the film industry, Muhammad Ali and Zeba. His office manager was also there. They were a group of five or six people who had made it to the border and my father got special permission and came up to the last point of the Pakistani gate. They were waiting there anxiously for me. We hadn't seen each other since I left Pakistan.'

Tina becomes teary-eyed as she says this, her voice rocking with emotion, 'From this side, unfortunately, the Indian officers weren't so sympathetic to the situation. They wouldn't allow me to go beyond a point. I was standing at the immigration point at the Indian side of the border but the officer was just so stubborn. He just wouldn't allow me to go and meet my parents. He kept saying I needed special permission from some ministry and so on and so forth. I hadn't met my father for so many years but he just wouldn't allow me to go to the gate. He simply refused.' She takes a deep breath, trying to gain her poise, 'Unfortunately, I didn't get to see them. A couple of months later my father had a heart attack and died.'

For the next few seconds neither of us speaks. I want to tell her how sorry I am to hear this but I know no words can make up for the aching loss she has had to bear; to have been so close to her father but not have been able to step forward, to hold him just one last time. After a quiet moment, she speaks again, 'That day I saw him from a distance. He was standing where the parade takes place and was waving at me. I could see all of them. He was trying his best to get the Pakistani officers to talk to the Indian ones about allowing me to come forward but it didn't work.'

As I swallow uncomfortably, I am reminded that despite all the beautiful stories I had heard about the border, about Naseer Ashiq's (Chapter One) father meeting his family at the *mela*, about mothers and daughters coming together at the Neelum River, also known as Kishanganga, about how

Muhammad Rauf (Chapter Two) was treated at the border by the Sikh officials, there is also the other reality of the border. The reality of separation and rupture, of distance and divide. No political reasoning or policy can rationalize the pain caused to Tina and the hundreds of other Pakistanis and Indians at the border. Their void cannot be filled by any diplomatic explanation or historical justification. Yes, it was at the border that Tina caught the last glimpse of her father, but it was also this border which prevented her from stepping forward, from embracing him one last time, from going home to her friends and family.

'It was a few years later, once I finally got my passport, that I was able to visit home. I was extremely nostalgic—every time I go back, even now, it's nostalgic for me. I still meet my school friends . . . Lubna . . . Rubina . . . I still have memories from my childhood, of my neighbourbood, of Diwali and Holi. I even remember the *chaatwala* and ice-cream*wala* near my house on Tariq Road,' she laughs.

In her own small way, Tina continues to strive for change, both personally and professionally. She has made sure that her husband Ravi, to whom she was married in the 1980s in Delhi, and her sons maintain a strong link with her family—consisting of her mother, brother and his wife—in Pakistan. Every year she ensures that her children spend time in Karachi, getting to know the city of their mother and grandparents. 'You know, Anam, I feel my insights of people from both sides gives me this unique ability to bring them together (through her organization Routes2Roots) with the sensitivity that others may not have.' But hasn't she faced any issues over the years? 'I've never had any issues. At times my friends tease me and say, "*yeh tou Pakistani hai.*" (She is a Pakistani.) When Pakistan and India are playing a cricket match, they'll bother me and say, "*Iski allegiance tou udhar hai.*" (Her allegiance is with Pakistan.) But this is all in good humour. I have wonderful friends in both countries,' she smiles.

But what about the intelligence agencies? Haven't they ever harassed her to find out whose 'side' she is really on, who she is loyal to? 'Never!' she answers, 'I think the Pakistanis take me as their own while Indians think I'm one of them. I swing both ways!' She lets out a hearty laugh and then says, 'When I meet people in the Pakistani High Commission in India they say, "*Oye ye te saddi kuri hai!*" (She's one of our girls!) I truly enjoy the love and affection from both sides. I often call Pakistan my *maika* (maiden home) and India my *sasural* (in-laws),' her voice echoes with a contagious mirth. She has found peace. She doesn't want just India or Pakistan, she wants both and they both want her.

I cannot help but think she has come full circle; that this was what her father had envisioned. That they would have the best of both worlds. For many this has failed to become a reality, but in the exception of Tina we find both India and Pakistan, rupture and bonds, divide and reunification. Her story leaves me wondering whether other divided families would have similar stories, whether they would have found eventual peace, some normalcy, in the midst of the absurdity of Partition.

chapter four

UNEASY COME, UNEASY GO
SHIREEN AND AMY

'We really belong to both places. We belong to the undivided subcontinent. I can't say I grew up here and went there. It wasn't really like that at all,' Shireen (the name has been changed to protect her identity) takes a deep breath, wrapping and unwrapping the ends of her beige sari around her left thumb. 'When I was required here, I was here. When I was required there, I was there and I would keep coming and going . . .'

'Although it wasn't easy to come and go,' Amy (the name has been changed to protect her identity) cuts in. 'No it never has been,' Shireen agrees softly.

I am sitting with two elderly sisters in their home in Defence Housing Society, Lahore. A few lanes away, McDonald's, Dunkin' Donuts and Subway proclaim modernity but sitting inside their sunny home, I am surrounded by old remnants, dating back almost a century. The over-sixty-year-old grandfather's clock from England, their father's rocking chair from what is now referred to as *old* Lahore, and the table in front of us, once upon a time intricately carved by woodworkers from Bombay, in their own little way keep alive the memories of the British Raj, the sense of belonging to both lands, to India as much as to Pakistan. Lahore and Bombay sit side by side, as does the Pakistani Amy next to her Indian sister, Shireen.

Shireen, in her early eighties, is the elder of the two sisters. Amy is twelve years her junior. They live here alone, as each other's only strength and support. But their warmth and hospitality means that they are often surrounded by friends and visitors from both Pakistan and India, two countries that they have spent most of their childhood crisscrossing. Despite an age difference of almost sixty years, Haroon and I have also been good friends with them for over a year now.

'For most people of my generation—I am eighty-five now—it has never been an either-or situation,' Shireen starts but is interrupted once more by the younger Amy, 'Although it's different for people of my generation. I have very much grown up post Partition. I have grown up in Pakistan. I don't have that kind of affinity with India.'

Born in Bombay in 1930, Shireen and her sister belong to the dwindling Zoroastrian community of Pakistan. Their mother was originally from Bombay itself, moving to Lahore after her marriage in 1925. Their father, however, was a true Lahori and at the time of Partition, leaving his city was simply unimaginable. 'Our father would have never shifted anywhere as this was where he had lived, his forefathers had lived; this was his home. He also believed that the politics of the state had nothing to do with us; that whether a Muslim or Hindu government was in place, we Parsis would remain unaffected. My mother, having married my father, also made this her

home.' Thus when August 1947 loomed around the corner
and families were packing away their lives in small boxes and
rolled-up cloth, this family of four, like Tina's (Chapter Three),
never thought about parting with their city. They were to
become a part of the changing landscape and character of
Lahore; a witness to the millions of migrants pouring in from
across the border, a spectator to the birth of a new state and
then to its transition to the Islamic Republic of Pakistan.

'It was a multicultural society back then. I used to have
Hindu, Muslim and Christian class fellows at the Cathedral
School and no one quite thought in terms of communities.
Everyone was a human being first, that was what was
important,' Shireen tells me. 'We would walk everywhere. My
mother and I would start from Waris Road, where we used to
live, and go all the way down to Jail Road where Kinnaird
College was. And later I'd cycle to the Sacred Heart College,
on my beautiful green Raleigh cycle, while my gardener huffed
and puffed behind me, trying to keep up,' she says, letting out
a chuckle, 'It was so safe and wonderful.'

I cannot help but compare this image with the conditions
in Lahore today. A girl walking on the street alone, regardless
of whether she is wearing a *burqa* or skinny jeans, evokes
curiosity. Men stare, grabbing their greasy beards in
amusement. The sight is a treat for them. For the female there
is no guarantee of safety. Many choose to not go out on their
own, increasing their dependence on the men in their lives.
This is my Lahore. It is my home, one that I wouldn't give up
for the world, but it is certainly not as safe as Shireen's was.

Luckily, she speaks again and I am forced to push my
disappointment to the backseat. For now I am to go back to
her world, here in the Paris of the East—as Lahore used to be

called—and in Bombay, which is as vivid for her; after all, she would visit the city with her family at least once a year. 'Did you know that Bom literally means beautiful? It is one of the most beautiful natural harbours, at least around the western coast of the subcontinent. Back then it wasn't as crowded as it is now. And there were none of these terrible slums. The population lived very comfortably within its own limits, as it were,' she sighs.

'It was altogether a very, very pleasant place . . . a very cosmopolitan and free society. Anyone could do anything they wanted; no one would bother to even stare. And the social life was lovely. There were lots of clubs, like the Gymkhana, and cultural activities, plays, concerts, singing, dancing were routine.' Every summer Shireen and Amy would board the Frontier Mail with their mother, which would take them from Lahore to their mother's maternal home in Bombay. 'It was a journey of about two nights and three days. The carriages were delightful, all with separate bathrooms attached. Families could travel by themselves or with a companion or two. I still remember the lovely cream of chicken soup we would order for our lunch or dinner . . .

'I think I was just about five at this time,' adds Amy, 'but I remember how wonderful it was just looking outside the window and stopping at the stations. There would be all this interesting food stuff and little trinkets. They would sell *bhel puri, channas, garam garam andey.* One would want to sample everything.'

Later, when the train would terminate at Bombay Central, the family would make their way to their grandparents' home, the Petit House. 'It was huge, from here to the end of the road,' Shireen says, stretching her arms wide to give me an idea of the length and breadth of the house. 'It was a one-storey house, with a long hallway and four huge rooms on each side. And each bathroom was as gigantic as the lounge we're sitting in!' she laughs, and Amy nods in agreement besides her. 'In the evenings, we would ride our horse Billie who lived in the stables and then our great-grandfather would take us down the Marine Drive in the Victoria carriage . . . it was such an honour!'

The fond memories have brought a smile on both their faces, slight but warm. They tell me that while these visits made for great childhood memories and overflowing family albums, for their mother, being able to be amongst her people struck another chord altogether. While her own husband and children were in Lahore, the link she had with Bombay could never be forgotten. 'Our mother was never able to let go of her emotional ties with the city and whenever we would go there she was so much more at ease, so relaxed over there.'

Partition, however, cut through not only the subcontinent but also created an irreparable divide in their family. 'Our mother felt a wedge had been built between her early life in Bombay and her life here in Lahore. Of course, she eventually reconciled with living here but emotionally she was always there, in Bombay, even until she died in 2004.' Like millions of others, she was to become a Pakistani overnight. Her home, her childhood, her ties were now in another land, a land which could not become foreign despite its best attempts to separate her, to deny her, to cast her out. But it was one that she could no longer claim either. 'We got so used to having all this furniture from Bombay in our house, from that portrait over there to those side boards and carved pieces, but whenever my mother would walk through this passage, she would say, "Where would those woodcarvers be now?" I think she always longed for her life in Bombay.'

Shireen, who was still a student at this time, did not feel the same loss as her mother. Lahore was where her school, her friends, her family were. For Bombay to now be a part of another country was a strange concept to grapple with but unlike her mother, it was not a truth she couldn't reconcile with. She would still visit, she thought; things would still be the same. But as she was to soon find out, Partition was going to have its own repercussions for her. Geared up to become a leading musician, the bloodshed and violence that ensued came to stand in the middle of the only future she had envisioned. Partition was threatening to abruptly halt her education.

'I was to appear for a music examination in 1947 in Lahore. But that year, the Trinity College of London said that they were sorry but they couldn't send an examiner here because of all the disturbances in Lahore. After all the preparation the thought of just not being able to appear was awful. I cried and cried and thought my life was going to be over. Eventually my parents couldn't bear it any longer and decided to send me to Bombay with a family friend; I was to appear for my examination there where the conditions were far better.'

Shireen's examination was right around the time of Partition when families were travelling in flocks from Pakistan to India and India to Pakistan. Conditions were horrible; trains would be stopped midway, passengers raped and sliced up. Going to Bombay at this time was life-threatening; far from the safe trips she had taken in the beautiful carriages of the Frontier Mail. This time no one was going to be allowed to look out of the windows to see the passing scenery; there would be no cream of chicken soup or *bhel puri* being sold at the station. Getting across alive was the only thing that mattered. When she got to the train station, Shireen saw that all the shutters were already down and that the passengers were sitting huddled together because of the threat of attacks. Fortunately, theirs was a lucky train, one that reached its destination unharmed, but as she says, 'Those were some of the most frightening hours of my life. None of us knew if we would get there alive. We just sat and prayed and prayed. We knew it was just a matter of fate; whether our train would be attacked or the one after . . . it was all about luck.'

Gambling with her life, Shireen finally reached Bombay and immediately moved into the Petit House. Here she practised for over eight hours a day, realizing the importance of passing the test after such an arduous journey. The practice paid off, for she topped the examination in India, Burma and Ceylon—what was later to be known as Sri Lanka. However, with one exam out of the way, Shireen soon had to face another hurdle. Her BA examinations in Lahore had been stopped due to Partition and she needed to appear for her history paper before December 1947 in order to graduate.

With the massive flood of migration on both sides of the border, trains and flights were packed, making it increasingly difficult for Shireen to find her way home. 'I had come to Delhi from Bombay but it was so difficult getting a flight to Lahore. They were just running shuttle flights so they had removed all the seats from the aircraft and people had to sit on their baggage. There was such a lot of transfer of population from Lahore to Delhi and Delhi to Lahore. The whole airport was strewn with people who had just arrived on a shuttle flight or were leaving. You had to walk over them to find out if there was any room on the flight. There was no ticket, no one had to pay anything.'

Reaching out for a glass of water beside her, she tells me, 'I had to go to the airport for three consecutive days before I could board the flight. My parents didn't even know where I was or if I would be able to make it in time for the exam.' That night, when she got home, she found her parents crouched by the fire. Her mother was silently weeping; she didn't know if she would see her daughter again.

'Those were very troubled times. There was so much misery around us that it was difficult to continue with our lives . . . but we all had to. I appeared for my exam that winter and I was given an honour by the Trinity College of Music in London. My family was ecstatic! It was the first piece of good news in months and we felt that it was the start of many wonderful things to come, that we would all be able to move on from the madness of Partition.' These thoughts were reaffirmed when she received the Fulbright scholarship allowing her to further her studies in music in the US in 1952. Shireen was ready to leave 1947 behind. There was much to look forward to.

But ten years are not enough to push the baggage of Partition to the corners of the past. The aftershocks of such an event are felt even decades afterwards. They are etched into the lives of the Partition generation; there is no forgetting 1947 for them. In Shireen's life, too, Partition had thrust its way back by 1957; it wanted to be the navigator of her destiny, to dictate the turn her life was going to take. 'I had come back from the States in 1955 and had started to work at the Home Economics College in the field of child education and development in Lahore. I was also running my own music show on Radio Pakistan. But news came in that I had to go to India to look after our family property and prevent it from being taken over by the Indian government. My father instructed me to go to Bombay immediately. I was supposed to become an Indian national, he told me. That was where I was going to live from now onwards.'

Shireen's father, like many other Zoroastrians, had assets in Bombay, a city which boasted of one of the highest population of Zoroastrians at that time. As the governments of Pakistan and India began to freeze non-Pakistani and non-Indian properties respectively, the family was afraid that their assets would be taken over by the state as enemy property. Being the eldest in the family, Shireen was to be sent to Bombay to take care of her family's possessions. 'I felt absolutely awful, my life as a pianist was conked off. And yet I was the only person; Amy was too young, and my parents couldn't leave, so there was only me left. We grew up being obedient to our parents so whether I liked it or not, I was sent off.'

She closes her eyes momentarily and I can tell that she is very sentimental speaking about this time, about her departure from her family. Beside her Amy, who is suffering from a chronic cold, begins to cough uncontrollably and excuses herself from the room. I wait until I feel Shireen has composed herself to talk further. She opens her eyes slowly and then says, 'But even leaving wasn't easy. It was 1957 by this time and it had become very difficult to cross the border. There were only two options: either you could go as a visitor or an immigrant. I didn't know which category I fit into. I ended up leaving Pakistan on a visitor's permit but entered India as an immigrant.' What an irony, I think. Just as their mother had to become a Pakistani, while Bombay burnt in her heart, Shireen had to become an Indian, far away from her cherished

Lahore. Both mother and daughter had been struck with the same fate; they were ruptured from their families, forced to take up a new nationality, to have their identities moulded, no questions asked, no choice given.

'It took three years to get a citizenship. All that time I was absolutely without any nationality at all. It was a horrible time, a really horrible time.' Touring government offices from Bombay to Delhi, Shireen found no one sympathetic to her cause. There were too many migrants to assist; she was just another number on the list. 'My situation was so common that when you went to the police and told them you were from Lahore, they wouldn't bat an eyelid.' Countless other people were making similar repeated trips to passport offices and high commissions in India and Pakistan to sort out who they were to become. People who simply belonged to the Indian subcontinent for centuries now had to determine which part of it they wanted to assert, where they wanted to belong more.

It was only when Raj Kumar College in Rajkot reached out to hire her that things picked up speed. 'I used to run a programme on Radio Pakistan by the name of *Twenty Centuries of Western Music* in collaboration with the first secretary of the British High Commission, Adrian Turner. When I was leaving for Bombay he asked me to meet the British Council folks over there and it was through them that I heard about Raj Kumar College. Since I had been working in education in Lahore at the Home Economics College, they thought I would be right for Raj Kumar College. The British Council representative in Bombay wrote to the principal and he immediately called me in to meet him. But that year my grandmother didn't let me fly to Rajkot because of the heavy monsoon rains and it was only when I was in Delhi a year later, chasing my nationality, that I decided to visit him.' Entering the campus, Shireen instantly fell in love with the college. Without a second thought she decided to take up the offer to be the headmistress of the junior section and it was from there, almost fifty years later, that she took retirement as principal.

'Once the principal took the matters in his hands, I had my immigration papers within a week's time and I was ready to become an Indian national for all legal purposes.' She tells me that as hard as it had been to give up her ambitions and her home in Lahore, she was fortunate that she had family in India, too. This was a familiar place, one where she had grown up and always felt at home. For her to become an Indian did not mean much more than a statement on an official document. She was already an Indian, she says, as much as she was Pakistani. What did a few signed papers have to do with that? Like Tina (Chapter Three), she was going to have two homes, she belonged to both places.

Unfortunately, however, the governments on both ends of the border do not feel similarly. For them individuals must choose which side they want to associate with; a blend of identities, of attachment, is not permitted. 'I was in Bombay during the 1965 war,' Amy says as she walks back into the room, with an extra layer draped over her *shalwar kameez*. 'I had gone to visit my grandparents for a few weeks in the summer but war broke out and I got stuck there; the plane services had been disrupted and discontinued. I was supposed to join Kinnaird College by September of that year, as a teacher, but I had to postpone that too.' I ask Amy what Bombay was like during the war. I have only ever heard stories from my parents and other relatives about the war in Lahore. The fighter jets, the trenches, the blackened windows; the sirens and the curfews. She tells me that in 1965 there was curfew in Bombay, too, a complete blackout. 'The windows would be covered with black paper and my cousins and I would spend the evenings with a recipe book, trying out new recipes because there was nothing else to do. It was a pity that being in the same country as my sister, we were still so far away from each other. Shireen was busy in Rajkot and couldn't get leave from the college at that time and because of my visa or permit— whatever it was—I had to be in Bombay. I wasn't allowed to travel to other cities.' Looking sideways at her sister, who is fighting hard to remain composed, Amy's voice too begins to quiver as she thinks back to those days. 'I remember I was constantly waiting to hear of the next flight home. I wanted to get back as soon as I could, to go back to my parents. I couldn't even speak to them during this time. We had to send messages via England or another third country and it was just really tough to be trapped like this, against one's wishes.'

While most people long for a visa for the other side, it is ironic that even after crossing the border, Amy could still not reunite with her sister. Just as Muhammad Rauf (Chapter Two) had to pass through Amritsar without being able to see his home or his people because of the 'type' of permission he held, Amy could not meet her sister despite being in that country. Such are the hostile policies between India and Pakistan, such is the distance between a Pakistani Amy and an Indian Shireen.

'When did you both meet next?' I ask them. 'I can't remember that really,' responds Shireen.'I know we hadn't seen each other for a few years and it was becoming increasingly difficult to visit Pakistan after the war. The planes had been stopped and the border had been sealed. But we had wanted to see each other so badly that finally my sister and I decided to meet in Kabul instead.'

'I had gone there earlier with my colleagues from Kinnaird College and it was such a lovely country, so very beautiful and peaceful then ... I wanted Shireen to see it,' says Amy, and Shireen tells me that she was thrilled to hear about this possibility. They were finally going to meet!

It is only when I look up from my notepad that I notice that Shireen's resolve has finally caved in. A few tears roll down her face and for the first time that day I realize that this isn't just a story I'm recording. This is the pain of separation, of not being able to connect, of going through so many obstacles to spend a few days with a loved one. What must it have felt like, after all the hurdles, the interruptions, to finally meet Amy? I cannot begin to imagine the uneasiness, the restlessness of those years, the uncertainty that must have gripped them. Would they ever see each other again?

'We spent quite some weeks there and it was just lovely. We caught up on so many things we had missed out over the years. She told me about her friends, about our mother and father, that we had moved out of our house on Waris Road. It was the first time in all those years that I felt complete, felt connected with my family.'

This trip was going to be the only relief for the next many years for both sisters. Much of the following decades were spent connecting, disconnecting and reconnecting with one another. Wars broke out, Indo-Pak relations were strained and Shireen and Amy, like countless others, suffered in the middle. When they were fortunate, Amy and her mother would visit Shireen in Rajkot and their relatives in Bombay.

Seldom, but sometimes, Shireen would get the visa to visit Pakistan for short but memorable trips. As she had thought, she was always welcomed in Lahore but the obstacles that stood in the way were exhausting, and always frustrating. 'It's been a nuisance,' Amy says, and just then the grandfather clock chimes, as if to signal its agreement. 'It has always been difficult, whether a permit, visa or passport. It has always been difficult to see her, to go to India or have her come here.'

'Don't forget the police reporting, dear,' Shireen adds. 'Yes,' agrees Amy, 'it takes away half the joy of the visit. If I'm in Delhi for two days, such a lot of time is wasted just reporting my entry and exit into and out of the city. It's just a hassle.'

Since 2000, when Shireen retired from Raj Kumar College, she has been living in Lahore on a vistor's visa. Her father was unwell and Amy was busy nursing her own husband. 'I was required at home.' Today, fifteen years later, Shireen longs to go back to Rajkot, to Bombay, to Bangalore, where her colleagues, her friends and relatives are. She has much work to wrap up too; she has wills to write, assets to give away, college work to finish off. As an Indian national, she can go back any time but her age no longer allows her to travel alone. Having remained unmarried, she needs Amy to accompany her as her support system. 'I have to go with her but I'm a Pakistani and it's not easy for me to get the visa. I submitted my application for the third time recently but each time they'd ask for something else, some other paper from India. Eventually, we just got our application back . . .' Amy says that she's planning on attempting to apply once more and I tell her that I will try to help. But I know the officials are unlikely to be moved by such a story. There is no room for emotions in Indo-Pak matters.

As the phone rings and Shireen reaches for it, Amy turns to me and says, 'It is so tough for her . . . it always has been. She is torn between Pakistan and India and it's not meant to be like that. Why can't they make it simple? Just let me take her there?' I don't have an answer to Amy's question, nor is she looking for one. Instead, I ask her what going to India means to her. She is far younger than Shireen and I remember that at the beginning of our conversation she had emphatically stated that India did not mean to her what it did to her sister. Sitting in her deep blue *shalwar kameez*, she repeats the same sentiment: 'I do share the friendship of her colleagues and friends there. I do have this closeness, but I don't have the same compulsion as she does. I basically go because she has to go. We also have relatives there and it's nice to be in touch with them but there is nothing more. My home, my friends, are here.'

Shireen is as Pakistani as she is Indian. It doesn't matter whether she holds a green or blue passport. It doesn't matter whether she has spent most of her life in India or that she is in Lahore right now. Both are home. But Amy is Partition's progeny. She can only belong to one land. It is an either-or situation for her. Her *shalwar kameez* contrasts with Shireen's sari, her memories are embedded in Kinnaird College and Lahore. Bombay is her birth place, Rajkot is where her sister's heart is, but her life is in Lahore. That is where she belongs.

'What I keep feeling is, you know, by being over there for so many years she really had to lose touch with what was going on here. There were very often incidents I know about and people I have close relationships with, and she doesn't know any of that. There are gaps and vice versa,' says Amy. From nearby Shireen hangs up the phone and shakes her head gently, her grey hair falling on her forehead. 'For the first twenty-five years, Amy knew practically nothing of my life. I also missed out on her growing up and her own career. I haven't seen any of the plays she has produced as a theatre artist. I wasn't even able to come home for the century celebrations of our Fire Temple in Lahore!' Clasping her hands together, she looks up at me, 'The division has totally destroyed our lives, to be frank, Anam. Partition created turmoil in our lives.'

We are all quiet for a while after she says this; there is a strange heaviness in the room, as if 1947 is still hanging above our heads. There is unity in this abode, Bombay and Lahore, Shireen and Amy, standing under one roof. Yet there is a divide, there is separation; visas are required to go home, permissions are needed but not granted. Travel plans remain incomplete; the crossing over even more difficult than it was sixty-seven years ago.

Shireen reaches out for my hand and says, 'Dear, we don't talk much about this because it's so traumatic. But it's important for people your age to know that at the personal level there is no hatred, no enmity. Bombay, Rajkot, Lahore are all home for me. The college gave me refuge at a time when I didn't even have a nationality, a passport, nothing. I can't abandon them, can I? And yet I belong to Lahore, too. I'm emotionally as tied to Lahore as my mother was to Bombay. It's sad that I need permission to remain here. This is my home as much as that is. Why must I choose?'

chapter five

SUSTAINING OLD BONDS

MALIK SIDDIQUI

I was taking one of my final driving lessons by the canal when my instructor, Omar, asked about my book. It is not customary for girls to learn driving from male trainers but my mother seemed to have more faith in them than their female counterparts. She had given into the sexist stereotypes—of how 'women simply didn't know how to drive', 'women don't make mistakes, they make blunders', and 'they're good drivers but they just get so lost in their thoughts'—despite driving around the streets of Lahore for the past four decades herself. It also wasn't common for one to make conversation with the instructors but Omar and I had hit it off from the beginning. He worked for the government of Pakistan, an employee of the Federal Bureau of Statistics, and taught driving early in the morning to make money on the side. With an inflation rate of around 8 per cent, nearly everyone was looking here and there to make ends meet. Plus, as he said, 'None of these government servants show up in office until 10 am. Instead, I can use these wee hours to put some extra bread and butter on the table for my family.'

Omar is also one of the few hardcore communists I have come across in Pakistan. Having garnered some support for his left-leaning politics in Sindh, his colleagues and he now try to attract Punjabis to their cause, hoping to launch their own political party in the next few years. Amidst our conversations about Marxism, minorities and democracy, we came to discuss my upcoming trip to India to attend a conference in Delhi.

Running CAP's Exchange-for-Change programme over the past two years, which connected Pakistani and Indian students through various communication channels, I knew enough to not discuss my perspective about the 'other' without being sure of who I was sitting around. People reacted in different ways when I told them we ran a project to link the youth of both countries. Many considered India an enemy state today, one that they saw no point in connecting with. A Pakistani brigadier I had recently conversed with had tried convincing me that 'they' were our enemies because an Indian UN official in Congo once offered him a glass of water while he was fasting, tempting him like Satan himself! I was about to ask whether it could have been a simple misunderstanding, if he forgot that it was Ramadan or wasn't sure if the brigadier sahib was fasting or not, but I was interrupted with something even more profound. 'Do you know, my own brother, an educated doctor, said to me the other day, "Bhai I've come to realize that Pakistanis and Indians share many similarities." Can you imagine that?' He nearly spat out in disbelief or venom; I wasn't sure which one it was nor did I want to find out. I backed down in my chair, smiled and took his leave. I didn't want to give the gentleman a cardiac arrest by telling him that I might just agree wholeheartedly with his brother.'

With Omar, however, I had established an understanding

over the past two weeks and so I excitedly shared what I expected from my second visit to India that year. Somewhere along the way, I also mentioned that I was trying to record the narratives of those Pakistanis who had crossed over or interacted with the so called 'other'. Omar was fascinated and the next day, when he came to pick me up at 6 am for my driving lesson, he was armed with a nomination in hand. This is how I was introduced to Malik Siddiqui (the name has been changed to protect his identity), a former government servant himself.

It is 24 July 2012 and, ironically, the month of Ramadan, as I make my way to Mr Siddiqui's house in Lahore's Model Town. The temperature has risen tremendously over the past few days and it doesn't seem like we are going to get any monsoon rain this year.

I am keeping rather unwell and have decided not to fast today but this is looked down upon by many conservative families nowadays in Pakistan. One cannot find a single restaurant open during the fasting hours and if you are caught eating or drinking on the road, you can be heavily penalized. Fortunately, grocery stores and bakeries are open for people to shop at and earlier in the day I had gone to one to buy myself some juice to take with my medicine. The gentleman behind the counter, however, saw my sleeveless clothes, mumbled a curse and then uttered, '*roza kharab kar diya hai*' (she has ruined my fast), before throwing the change back at me with a warm box of Nestle orange juice. To him, I was a Western girl with no morals or religion; I was not only trying to arouse him by my bare arms during the sacred hours of the

fast but I was also not fasting myself. I wondered if he stopped
to think that Islam offered much relaxation in terms of fasting,
to those who were too young or old, pregnant or ill. Of course,
it also did not cross his mind that there were 3 per cent
minorities living in the country, upon whom fasting was not
obligatory. But I suppose he was too preoccupied with his
'ruined' fast to contemplate anything else.

And so, when Mr Siddiqui asks if I would like to drink
something, I take one glance at him and Mr She-Ruined-My-
Fast comes to my mind. Mr Siddiqui is wearing a white *shalwar
kameez* with a matching skull cap and beard to support his
religious attire. The greying hair that lines his face can be
clenched in a fist, just as per the teachings of the Holy Prophet
(Peace be upon him). His family and he are busy preparing for
Umrah, for which they are meant to leave tomorrow. The Kaaba
(House of Allah) situated deep inside Saudi Arabia awaits
them. I am convinced that he must be awfully conservative
and would judge me even more than the shopkeeper. I thus
politely decline and then watch in horror as he takes a sip of
water while I sit parched. 'I'm unwell, so please excuse me,' he
says with a smile. If only I had done the same!

Realizing I was too quick to label, I ease slightly and adjust
myself on his maroon sofa. I am still taking out my notebook
and pen when a lady wearing a floral print *shalwar kameez* walks
into the room. 'Meet my daughter-in-law, Shabnam' (the
name has been changed to protect her identity). Shabnam, a
mother of three, is a sweet charming lady, probably in her early
thirties. Preoccupied with tomorrow's flight, she only sits with
us for a few minutes before sweating her way through the
house, packing and taking care of her children's countless
demands. She has heard that I am here to speak with her

father-in-law about India, about how his immediate family still lives there. She decides to take this time to tell me about her own links with the country. She has been to India too.

'My *nani* (maternal grandmother) was from Delhi but I never really spoke to her about it, although now I wish I had. And so when I went to India I didn't know much about it, apart from the occasional Bollywood movie here and there.' She looks sideways at Siddiqui before continuing, 'Of course, *Abba* had told me about his family over there. He said it was good but that's all I really knew.'

Shabnam visited India for the first time in 2004. She was accompanied by her in-laws. Crossing over into Amritsar, they were welcomed by a Sikh family who were family friends of her in-laws and wanted to make sure their transit was made comfortable. She tells me that they exhausted all hospitality in hosting them. Then too it was Ramadan and they arranged for a grand *aftari* for Shabnam and her family before safely transporting them to their next destination, Chandigarh. Here she stayed with Siddiqui's sister and her husband's *phupho* (paternal aunt), who is a minister in the government. 'I attended five *shaadis* while I was there! You know, Indian weddings are much more extended than our Pakistani ones. I also heard that the girl's side has to spend a lot of money. Sometimes the *baraat* even comes and stays overnight!' She is overly excited, her voice bubbling as she speaks about her trip. 'I also went to Nagina, my in-laws' ancestral home. Over there I saw their homes, the old *haveli*-type homes with huge *sehans*—verandahs.' As one of her children clings to her *dupatta*, she gets up to feed her. 'Have you ever been to India?' she asks, and before I can respond, she interjects, 'You should go. The people are so friendly. The shopkeepers were so happy to hear

we were from Pakistan! They would open their whole shops to
us, serving us *chaat* and fresh juice, as we sifted through hundreds
of colourful fabrics, the kind you cannot find anywhere here!'
Looking at her father-in-law, she says, 'It was a wonderful
experience *Abba,* I'd love to go again someday.'

Siddiqui chuckles as she leaves the room. 'You know, she
was scared before she left. She would ask me if the common
people would be nice to her knowing she was from Pakistan.
She would say, "Abba, I've heard all kinds of horrible stories
about Indians." And now look at her! One trip and she can't
stop talking about how great it was. She brought hundreds of
shopping bags back with her!'

Siddiqui himself was born in Nagina, Uttar Pradesh, on 27
March 1934. It was here that he lived until the early fifties,
when he decided to leave his family behind for Pakistan, all on
his own. Our conversation kicks off with talking about his
village at the time of Partition, an occurence which he spent
many of his waking hours fighting for. Siddiqui tells me that
with a total population of 30,000, Nagina hosted about 13,000
Muslims in 1947. 'The Congress had a strong control over the
area,' Siddiqui begins, and tells me that his own family was
involved in the larger political scenario of that time. His *taya,*
paternal uncle, was an MP from the Congress Party while
another uncle was a minister in the government. However,
since childhood, Siddiqui was an ardent supporter of the
Muslim League, despite his family favouring the Congress.

'I was about thirteen at that time and would attend all the
Muslim League rallies. My Muslim friends and I would yell
out slogans and organize student movements across the village
to garner support.' Walking through the streets with their
arms raised in the air and fists tightened, they would scream:

'"*Le ke rahenge Pakistan, bat ke rahega Hindustan.*" (Hindustan will have to split, Pakistan must be created!) "*Maareinge, mar jayenge, seene par goli khayenge, Pakistan banayenge.*" (We will kill, we will be killed, but we will create Pakistan).'

As August 1947 came closer, Hindu-Muslim rivalry also intensified. The divide, which was imminent, was inevitably going to show its colours in one way or the other. He was studying in the seventh grade when a Hindu boy insulted Pakistan. The Pakistan movement was at its peak at this time and Siddiqui was already at the forefront amongst the active youth. 'One day my class fellow, Namu Narayan, began to mock me, saying he would never let Pakistan become a reality, that the word was a curse. This made me furious.' Without a rational thought, Siddiqui grabbed the pen he was writing with and stabbed Narayan's hand. As blood began to pour out of Narayan's palm, the Hindu boys collected around them and began attacking Siddiqui. Dragging him by his collar, they took him to the Hindu headmaster who immediately broke branches of a nearby mulberry tree to beat him up. It was after a couple of thrashes that Siddiqui managed to cry out and tell the master that Namu had provoked him. Fortunately for him, the insanity of Partition had not yet caught up with his teacher and upon hearing this he threw the branches at the Hindu boys and asked them to never repeat what they had done. But I am told that such instances were not unprecedented in the Partition days.

Hearing this one would assume that Siddiqui had wanted to leave his ancestral home like millions of others who had to flee because of the tensions and the subsequent violence. But Siddiqui's relationship with Nagina and Pakistan is more complicated than that. He was not pro-Pakistan because he had to be; in fact, it was just the opposite. His family had a stronghold in the area and was well-settled. Regardless of the Hindu-Muslim divide, it shared an exceptionally cordial relationship with the community. Siddiqui himself was friends with more Hindus than Muslims. He tells me that they would play together and visiting each other's homes was routine. At Eid and Diwali they would exchange sweets and at weddings, they would exhaust all resources to help their neighbours, regardless of their religious beliefs.

This is similar to the pre-Partition life Muhammad Rauf (Chapter Two) from Sahiwal and Viqar Ahmad (Prologue) from Meerut had described to me and would also resonate in many of the other interviews during the course of my research. Whether the utopian reflections were truly representative of life before 1947 is debatable; was life really as harmonious or did it seem better in retrospect? As a researcher, six decades after Partition, this is something I cannot answer. But perhaps, memory and how people choose to remember certain events is as important as historical facts themselves. As Urvashi Butalia mentions in her book *The Other Side of Silence*, 'There has been considerable research to show that memory is not ever "pure" or "unmediated". So much depends on who remembers, when, with whom, indeed to whom, and how. But . . . the way people choose to remember an event, a history, is at least as important as what one might call the "facts" of that history, for after all, these latter are not self-evident givens; instead, they too are interpretations, as remembered or recorded by one individual or another.'[5]

I ask Siddiqui how his Hindu friends reacted to his support

---

[5]Butalia, Urvashi, *The Other Side of Silence*, Penguin Books, 1998, p.10.

for an independent country, which was going to not only split their nation but also take away many of their loved ones. He shakes his head and responds, 'The Pakistan movement never affected these relations . . . yes, at times you had petty fights between students and shopkeepers, but even when full-fledged violence broke out in the late forties and Hindus and Muslims were attacking each other outside, we remained friends and extended a helping hand to our neighbours as they did to us.'

But this hospitality was not enough for Siddiqui. He had been part of the movement for Pakistan and wanted it to become a reality not just for the Muslims but for himself too. It did not matter if no one was asking him to leave; it did not matter if he was still welcome in India. For him, Pakistan was where he belonged. It was what he had struggled for. And so, at the age of seventeen, while he was enrolled in his second year at Mustafa Municipal College, he decided to drop out and board the train to what he believed was the Muslim haven, and his rightful place to be.

'It was 1952 and my family had thought my fervour would have dampened by now. It wasn't that they did not support Pakistan but they had their business, their lives fully settled in India and they never thought about leaving. But I told them that if they did not let me go with their love and blessings, I would simply run away.' With this mindset and his parents fearing the lengths he could go to, he made preparations to leave for the country that he had fought tooth and nail for. Saying goodbye to his parents, siblings, friends and neighbours, he decided to travel to Pakistan through the Khokhrapar border at Tharparkar, Sindh. 'A train used to run between India and Pakistan to transport migrants. At this time you didn't need a visa or any other official documents. You just crossed over. The station was near my school and I had spent a lot of time there, volunteering to help those who were making their way to Pakistan. I would make milk bottles for the children, bring food for families, help them pack their belongings, so I knew the drill. I knew what I had to do to get to Pakistan.'

Siddiqui was young and the heat of the movement was burning inside him but the journey was not going to be easy. From Nagina he took a train to Delhi from where he crossed Rajasthan, Marwar, and Monabao before reaching Khokhrapar on 19 August 1952. 'Monabao is the last station of India. From there you have to walk about 12 kilometres to reach Khokhrapar. Once I got there I was exhausted. It had been twelve days since I had left home.'

For the next few weeks, Siddiqui lived in the refugee camps that were scattered across the border. Here he registered his Pakistani identity and became a national, living amongst hundreds of fellow migrants. But his next steps were clear to him: each week a goods train would pass by and take passengers to Hyderabad from where they would go onwards to other cities; one day Siddiqui sat on it, ready to depart for his final destination: Lahore, where one of his uncles was settled. 'I was so happy and proud of myself on having accomplished my dream, to be in Pakistan. Nothing can explain what I felt . . . I was in my land. This was my home.' That is how thousands of other Muslims felt too. The losses they had to bear to get here, the families that were left behind, the loved ones that were brutally murdered, could never be forgotten. But to inhale the air of the country they had fought for was some salvation. In such a situation, where they had no houses or families to call their own, the nation itself became their only home.

Siddiqui spent the next few months learning typewriting at the famous Young Men's Christian Association (YMCA). With its global motto of 'empowering young people', the skills Siddiqui learnt at YMCA indeed helped him. He started off his career as a typist at the Punjab secretariat and was later hired by the Federal Bureau of Statistics.

'How did you stay in touch with your family over the years?' I ask, and he tells me that for the initial few years they would write letters to each other and eventually, in 1955, he got a passport and went back to visit his village and its people for the first time. 'There was absolutely no issue like there is now. The deputy high commissioner's office was on Mall Road, right next to Scotch Corner. I submitted my application there and within two-three days, I had my visa.' Today, the Indian High Commission in Pakistan requires a minimum of forty days to process the visa application. Even then there are no guarantees and the majority, like Naseer Ashiq (Chapter One) from the border village in Kasur, returns empty-handed. But for Siddiqui at this time the reality was very different. With the visa in hand, he decided to cross over the Wagah border on foot and take the train to Nagina.

'I was very happy to see my family again. It had been three years and the separation wasn't easy but there was also no other choice for me. My family was here but my home was in Pakistan.' Siddiqui's story is interesting, to say the least; he is one of those migrants who migrated by choice. He left his house, his family behind of his own volition. And yet, he has ensured that he sustains the relations he has across the border, not just with his relatives but also with his friends and teachers, most of whom are Hindu and Sikh. This is important to him. Pakistan may be home but the relationships that matter, the memories that he cherishes, are all embedded somewhere deep inside India.

'The first time I went there my friends were so happy to see me; they all came to my house with *mithai* and we sat in the verandah for hours, discussing everything that had happened in our lives since I had left. Some of my friends were getting married by this time and others were leaving Nagina for better education. It felt strange to have missed out on that and especially that they couldn't relate to anything I was doing, but they were so welcoming, they treated me so well that I didn't feel like I wasn't a part of them anymore. We still mattered to each other.'

After this trip Siddiqui made it a point to visit Nagina every six months. While he was beginning to build a home and a family for himself in Pakistan, the one that was left behind in India always pulled him there. There was much to go back for. 'A few years later I visited again and went to see my old teacher, Gopinath. Upon seeing me he yelled in excitement and said: "What good timing! My daughter is getting married; my son, you must do her *ruksati*."' The *ruksati,* which means the departure of the bride from her home into that of her husband's, is one of the most sentimental and important rituals of a South Asian wedding. It is usually carried out by parents or very close relatives. To ask Siddiqui to perform the *ruksati* for his daughter, Gopinath had given him immense respect. There was no greater way to welcome him, to make him feel a part of the family.

Over the years, Siddiqui has called many of his relatives, including his siblings and cousins, to Pakistan. He says that they love it here. 'They shop like anything! They're even friends with the shopkeepers who give them discounts and they have discovered their favourite restaurants where they make me take them for *pai* and *nihari*.' Smiling, he adds, 'You know it is great, having one house there and one here. We consider ourselves lucky—we have two homes.' This is the first time that Siddiqui has used the word 'home' to refer to Nagina and I can't help but ask him if that is what it is for him. 'Of course, it is,' he replies instantly. 'When all the people you love are in one place, what else would you call it? I have a family here and one there and I may choose to live in one place because of my beliefs but my heart is in both. They are both home.' This is the reality for many from the Partition generation. Families are split between the two lands, both India and Pakistan are their abode. There is no clear line for these people; it is difficult to decipher what they love more, where they belong more. This confusion is the only truth for them.

I ask Siddiqui how India has changed over the years, in between the visits that he has made. 'There has been a lot of development, a lot of progress. But what is nice is that my home and its people are the same. Our *haveli*, which is situated in Mohalla Qazi, has been split between my brothers but it is still made of the same bricks my father laid down years ago. The people too, not just those in my village, but Indians generally, across cities, give us so much respect.' In June 1979, Siddiqui was crossing over the Wagah border with his seven-year-old son. As soon as the immigration officer on the Indian side saw his No Objection Certificate (NOC), he left all his work and quickly completed the customs and procedures, allowing him to sit in the train at the earliest. When Siddiqui thanked him for this gesture, he held up his hand in protest, 'Please don't thank me, sir. Your NOC shows that you're a government servant. It does not matter whether you are from India or Pakistan, we respect you equally.'

But while there is affection and continuity in bonds on one side, the poison of the Indo-Pak divide does not spare the best of us, especially those who try against all odds to sustain their link with what is now the enemy. The days of obtaining the visa easily in Lahore are over. Trips to Islamabad have to be made, money spent, queuing up required. Delays are unavoidable, exceptions are rarely made. The harsh policies between India and Pakistan finally caught up with Siddiqui too. 'I was unable to make it for my parents' funerals. I didn't have the visa to go. I was their son and I couldn't go . . . both for my mother and father.' Travel to India can no longer be sudden. Plans have to be made in advance. There is no room for emergencies, for impulsive visa applications. Death is too unexpected; there is no section for it in the application form, there can be no urgent processing, at least for the ordinary people. Today Siddiqui's parents are buried in India, miles away from him. This is the price he has had to pay for his country. 'You have to fight a constant struggle every day, to visit, to be one with them. I don't regret my decision but I had never realized how much I would have to give up for Pakistan. I had no idea that things would ever become so bad.'

In 1999 when Siddiqui was on his way to India, the Kargil conflict erupted. Immediately all transport between India and Pakistan was halted. He was mid-way, travelling by bus, when he was informed about the escalated conflict. Just in time, officials rushed Siddiqui and other travellers back to Pakistan by plane. But this wasn't the end of it. In 2001, when the Indian Parliament in New Delhi was attacked by terrorists linked to Pakistan, tensions between the two countries rose to new heights. The Indian government passed orders that all Pakistanis should go back and Siddiqui had to cut his travel short, rushing back from one home to the safety of the other. The decisions taken at the top level, the fights that break out between the governments, have repeatedly affected Siddiqui, as they affected Tina (Chapter Three) and Shireen (Chapter Four).

'It is also difficult for my children to visit,' he tells me, his voice frustrated. 'They say that their immediate family is in Pakistan, what need or association do they have to visit?' His children are second-generation Pakistanis. What link could they have to India? These questions are repeatedly asked by officials. Visiting grandparents or uncles does not sit well with them.

Upon my most recent visit to India in August 2012, I was to take the Pakistan Tourism Development Corporation (PTDC) bus back to Lahore. While the bus was scheduled to leave for Lahore at 6 am, passengers had been advised to arrive two hours early for security clearance. With my experience of non-punctual taxi drivers in Lahore, I booked a cab an hour in advance to avoid any delays in reaching the bus terminal. To my surprise, the driver arrived 15 minutes earlier than requested and then sped through the empty streets of Delhi, reaching the Ambedkar bus terminal much before I had expected. Here, I was greeted with pitch darkness, an empty station and a locked gate. Frantic, I tried to dial the number on my bus ticket, only to be greeted by a sleepy gentleman on the other side. 'It's 3 am. We will only open the gate at 4 am, Ma'am. Beep.' My taxi driver was getting impatient and so I reached for my bags to step out but being from Lahore, I knew the streets of Delhi could be no safer for a girl in the middle of the night. Instead, I sat back in the seat and decided to offer the driver whatever little Indian currency I had left on me and asked him to let me stay indoors. We made brief conversation about the BJP and the Congress Party, his home and Old Delhi. He was fascinated to hear that I was from Lahore, and even more surprised to learn how similar it was to his Delhi. The time passed before I knew it and by 3:45 I saw other passengers slowly make their way towards the terminal.

After I had my bags checked, I was approached by the porter, who asked me to pay for his services. I couldn't believe I had forgotten this when I generously handed over all my remaining Indian currency notes to the taxi driver outside. All I had now was some Pakistani change. He stared at my face blankly, his hand spread out in front of me. Not knowing what to do, I turned sideways and found an elderly woman standing next to me. I asked her if I could give her some Pakistani currency in return for a little Indian change. A younger lady, presumably her daughter, came forward and smiled. 'Don't worry, take this.' For the rest of the journey, we stayed together. They were a family of four—grandmother, daughter and her two children.

As we had the tea and biscuits offered at the bus terminal, the grandmother and I began to talk. She had been married off to her cousin at Partition and sent to Pakistan to make a home for her and her husband's family. The rest of her family, including her siblings and parents, remained in Jalandhar, India. She has often visited them over the years but now, at her age, it is becoming more and more difficult to do so. She needs someone to accompany her. 'But it isn't easy, you know. My visa comes through but not for the rest of my family. They say, "They haven't visited before, why this interest now? What connection do they have with India?" Even this time, my grandson and I had simple visas but my daughter and granddaughter had police reporting ones and so we had to spend hours in Indian police stations, registering our entry and exit.' I could relate to this for during my two-week trip I had reported my entry and exit four times in Delhi and twice in Mumbai. Each report had taken hours away from my limited time in India. This is the situation for many other Indians and Pakistanis too. Selective visas are issued, reporting needs to be done in every city; questions are asked about personal affinity and affiliation, suspicious officials follow passengers. Families cannot travel as families. The divide carves its way in there too.

The door creaks open and Shabnam peeps in, announcing that it is almost *aftari* time. Her entry breaks my chain of thought and brings me back to Siddiqui's family room, where we have been sitting over the past hour or so. Outside, the temperature is beginning to cool as the time for *magrib* prayers approaches. 'You must have *aftari* with us,' Shabnam says. There are still about 45 minutes left for that so I decline her offer. I can tell the family is busy today and I have probably overextended my stay.

Before I get up, Siddiqui reaches for the cordless phone by his side and dials a number he seems to know by heart. A moment later, I realize he is speaking with his sister Farzana, settled in Chandigarh. He gives the phone to Shabnam who excitedly tells her about her Umrah plans, promising to pray for her while she is there. Then she asks Farzana to visit Pakistan, '*Programme banayen jaldi Pakistan aney ka.*' From the other side, I can tell that Farzana is doing the same. She is inviting Shabnam to come spend summer and winter vacations with her family. Siddiqui looks at me and smiles, 'On one hand the restrictions are greater than they ever were and on the other hand you are so much more connected. *Jab chahein baat kar lein* (We can talk whenever we want).' I smile back at him and take my leave. Today social media and direct phone lines have connected several families. Until now, this process has gone uninterrupted. As I walk back to my car, anxious for a sip of water, I can only hope that this connectivity is not short-lived; that more families are not separated, that more burials do not have to take place without loved ones, that wars do not snap off relationships, that more people are not caught in between.

PART III

RECLAIMING HERITAGE

A MUSEUM OF MEMORIES

chapter six

LETTING GO

ROSHAN ARA

'Like every other year, we had gone up to the mountains for the summer in May '47.' Roshan Ara Begum, one of Pakistan's leading choreographers, was only thirteen years old then. Born in Aligarh, Roshan Ara spent much of her childhood travelling between what is now India and Pakistan. Trekking behind her father, who was the chief minister of Kapurthala and was posted variously in Kapurthala, Jaipur and Ambala, the family finally settled in Lahore during the 1940s. In 1947, as per the annual tradition, the family had decided to go up to Kashmir to spend summer vacations. 'Everybody used to do that at that time. Even my friends, many Hindus, had come up with their parents.'

Hailing from a family that celebrated the arts, Roshan Ara and her sisters routinely put up shows for their relatives and friends on these trips. This year was no different but the occasion had made their performance even more important. The subcontinent was gaining freedom from the British Raj. There was much to celebrate. It was as she huddled together

with her friends—Christian, Hindu and Muslims alike—
preparing skits and dances to entertain the public, that the
quest for a separate nation, for Pakistan, reached a new
momentum. 'Sitting here we were completely cut off from the
brutal real world. We children had no idea about what was
going on. Here Hindus and Muslims were standing together,
preparing to put up a show to honour our freedom from the
British when outside the same Hindus and Muslims were
slitting each other's necks.'

While the children danced and sang together, Roshan Ara's
mother, Mehmooda Jehan Begum, had already made her way
to Karachi to follow her leader's footsteps. 'She was an avid
Muslim Leaguer, a freedom-fighter,' Roshan Ara explains. 'A
few days before Partition she had taken the train to Karachi,
where Quaid-e-Azam Muhammad Ali Jinnah was preparing
for the creation of Pakistan. Little did we know, the rioting
had started while we were enjoying our summer vacations and
my mother ended up getting her entire back burnt in a bomb
blast in that train. It was then that she realized how bad the
situation was. She rushed back to us and was horrified that we
were still putting up a show. I still remember she said, "Look
at the trouble outside and here Muslims and Hindus are
celebrating together. Come on, hurry up, we must leave at
once!"'

Panic stricken, the family quickly packed up their belongings
and decided to leave for Lahore right away.

'When we got to our home in Lahore, all my Hindu friends
had already left. Their houses were empty. I never saw most of
them again.' Luckily, the area in which Roshan Ara lived—
Birchwood Road off Jail Road—did not face much violence
but while the children were instructed to stay indoors, Muslim
looters came and raided their friends' homes.

'We lived in our house in Lahore until the '60s but the landscape had totally changed after Partition. It just didn't look the same without all my friends, with new people in their homes. And then when school reopened after summer vacations, seeing the empty desks and chairs was very difficult to process as a child. The atmosphere was markedly different and the idea of never seeing my friends again didn't settle well with me.' Roshan Ara found her Lahore altered. The new faces and the crowded streets brought a strange unfamiliarity with them. The battered bodies, helpless refugees and desperate faces had sucked away the soul of Lahore. The state of their city was so deplorable that even their struggles for a separate homeland seemed futile. What had they fought for? How were they to move on?

While everyone dealt with the mixed emotions—the happiness of attaining their own country meshed with feelings of loss, nostalgia and anguish—Roshan Ara and her friends decided to volunteer at a refugee camp based in Forman Christian College. They did not want to sit around helplessly. They wanted to salvage whatever little was left of their Lahore, of the people that had poured in from across the border in appalling conditions. 'We were thirteen-fourteen-year-old girls with no training but we did the best we could. There were just one or two trained nurses and a handful of doctors. The rest were all volunteers like us, young students and housewives. We would pick out maggots from the wounds of refugee families, cleaning and bandaging them ... it was horrible. People were dying everywhere, families were refusing to take back abducted women, there was no food, clothing. Lahore was in a state of utter despair. It looked nothing like it used to.'

Noticing how upset she is talking about Partition, I decide to change the topic. Many times the people I speak to about 1947 begin to cry and break down. It is a wound entrenched in each one of them. Some bear the physical scars of the violence; others have the bloodshed engraved in their minds. I had recently spoken to an elderly lady about her Partition experience for the CAP Oral History Project. She shared terrible scenes from the refugee camps in Delhi; about the slaughter, rape and kidnappings. Talking about this upset her so much that she lost consciousness. For the next many days, she only spoke about the corpses and the brutality she had witnessed over six decades ago; it had pulled her back into a horrific past that the Partition generation tried hard to avoid. Scared about a similar reaction, I ask Roshan Ara to tell me more about her father's postings in what is now India, about what her life was like prior to this bloody split. Her expressions soften instantly and she gives me a warm smile, her eyes crinkling at the corners. For the past twenty years Roshan Ara has been teaching dance at the Art Council in Lahore. Sporting shoulder-length hair and a petite frame, she is one of the few people in the country who has not only excelled at Kathak and Bharatnatyam forms of dance but has also taught folk performances to students from all over the country. At the age of eighty-one, she is possibly one of the most vibrant people I have come across.

'I was born in Aligrah. That's where my grandparents lived for a long time but we would keep moving around, wherever my father went,' she begins. 'We spent a lot of time in Jaipur, Lahore, Kapurthala, Ambala. And then, of course, we would visit the hill stations whenever we had vacations.' With so many stories to tell, Roshan Ara is a woman of a few words.

She provides short and precise answers and it is only with a lot of probing that one can encourage her to give away a little more. I ask her to tell me about these places, about her memories from this time, and hope that she is willing to share the anecdotes, the recollections, however vague they may be. 'I was very young but I still remember how royal and regal the maharaja of Kapurthala was. He had a zebra carriage which fascinated us children. It was used as a ride for the guests and the zebras were trained in such a way that they would only run when the trainer asked them to!' she lets out a giggle, making me forget that she is close to my grandmother's age. 'But that is really all I remember from there.'

She stops once more but I remain persistent and ask her how she would spend the rest of her time as a child, hoping to jog her memory. This has been my experience with many of the people I have interviewed. The horror stories come forward quickly, the others are often pushed behind. Perhaps it was because that is what they were asked to repeat more often, those were the stories that fit the conventional understanding of Partition, popular in society. Perhaps it was because those brutal incidents had overpowered the other memories. In a conversation I had with a friend and psychotherapist, Jasmyn R. Khawaja, she spoke of her experience working with trauma victims. Describing trauma memories as emotion-based, she said, 'Often the most vivid memories these victims recall are fuelled with strong emotions such as fear or shock, etc. These traumatic memories are so dominant that people can often not remember events that occurred directly, before or after the trauma. A kind of disassociation sets in as part of a survival mode in which less emotionally charged details get overshadowed by the threatening ones.'

My probing works somewhat and Roshan Ara tells me, 'My father was posted in Kapurthala but we were put in school in Lahore. So it was only on the weekends that he would take us to Kapurthala. I still remember our house there . . . it was right opposite the palace and it had these absolutely wonderful grounds . . . side lawns, front lawns, rose gardens. I would take my friends along on some weekends and we would put up shows over there. As I grew older I missed our house a lot but as children you forget easily, and my sisters and I quickly took to the new cities our father took us to.' Slowly, she is starting to say more and I want to keep up the momentum. 'Tell me about these other places, please.'

'Well, I have a lot of memories from Mussoorie. I attended convent school over there for some time and I remember how beautiful it was!' Excited to talk about those days, she happily tells me how lovely the city was, located in the middle of the hills. 'The children used to ride horses up and down after school and there was even a skating rink where all of us would go.' The convent where Roshan Ara studied had morning mass and all the children would go to the chapel to say their prayers. While she knew these hymns by heart, her mother also made sure that the children read the Quran and offered their prayers at home. 'Such was the difference between home and school,' she remarks as she excuses herself from the room.

When she walks back in a moment later, she is holding a stack of black and white photographs of Chevrolets, horses and grand houses. Sitting down beside me, she says, 'There used to be a lot of restaurants in Mussoorie. We would go and eat piping hot potato balls and in the evenings, sometimes, our parents would take us to see ballroom dancing. Some of my best memories are from there.' Looking down at her lap she

takes me through the snapshots of hills and meadows, stretching
far across. In one such picture, I can see a group of four young
girls sitting in a lawn. 'This one is from Jaipur,' she says, 'that is
my sister right there and that's me next to her. My house there
was very grand too. It had tennis courts, a swimming pool,
these huge gardens . . . a vegetable garden, a rose garden, a
front lawn. My father was serving as the chief minister of the
Kapurthala state and worked closely with the maharaja, I
remember as a child I used to stare at his maharani. Her name
was Ayesha and I used to just keep looking at her, completely
in awe. She used to dress up just like a princess.'

Inspired by the royalty, here too Roshan Ara and her sisters
put up plays for their parents and friends. One of her elder
sisters would write humorous dramas whereas the others would
perform. 'There was no TV or any other entertainment so
these performances were the highlight. I remember our
grandma's sister used to get so angry. She was quite conservative
and would say, "You have a new brother-in-law and you're
making young girls dance in front of him!"' she laughs, 'but
those were really good times. There was a lot of freedom, a lot
of encouragement of the arts.'

In 2000, when Roshan Ara had a chance to travel to Jaipur
with her husband, she was delighted to be back in the city
where she had spent so much time. 'Unfortunately we were
only there for a day and I didn't know the address so I couldn't
go see my house but all the memories just came rushing back
to me. I went and saw the beautiful Hawa Mahal where the
wife of the maharaja used to live. It's now a tourist spot and
anyone can go in but back then I remember there used to be so
many doors because the concept of *purdah* (veil) was very strict.
They were so particular about these things. You know, the

servants weren't even allowed to turn their backs towards the maharaja or maharani? They would bow and move backwards in respect.'

I ask Roshan Ara if she found the city altered, different from what she had expected, but she shakes her head. 'It hasn't changed much. The walls are still pink as they used to be. It's just that there is a lot more traffic and the palaces have been converted into hotels!' One of my friends had recently told me about one such hotel, the Rambagh Palace. It was known to be the maharani's residence but today those who can afford it spend a night or two there. This regal experience costs them over 27,000 Indian rupees per night. Yet regardless of how much one pays, it is unlikely that the royal lifestyle that Roshan Ara and her sisters were able to witness first-hand at such a young age can be bought with any amount of money today. Perhaps this explains her posture; there is a touch of grace and elegance in the way she sits and speaks.

Seeing her in a good mood, I decide that now is probably the right time to ask about her Hindu friends, about the time spent with them before that fateful summer of 1947. 'I made my closest friends while I was studying at Queen Mary's College in Lahore,' she says. 'At that time there were a maximum of four or five Muslim girls in my class, the rest were all Hindus or Christians. Even our principal was an English lady, a very strict woman, mind you! But I have very happy memories from my days at school. The friends I made there are still my friends today. They're not all alive and those who aren't in the best of health but we still share a very strong bond.' She clasps her hands together as she says this as if to show me how tightly knit her relationships are, and before I can ask her where most of these friends are now, she starts speaking again. I haven't seen her so talkative all afternoon and sit back so that she can continue. 'There was a lot of emphasis on extracurricular activities, especially sports. My sister was a tennis champion and I was very good at hockey. But of course studies were important too. We only didn't like geography. In fact, all the children hated it. It was just terrible,' she chuckles. 'We would run away from it until Ms Penny, this English teacher, came to teach it. We just fell in love with her.'

For the next few minutes, Roshan Ara talks about cycling to school and coming back in her family's yellow-coloured Chev if she was lucky; otherwise she and her sisters would sit on tongas and make their way home. She tells me about the *halwa puri* she would buy for a few *aanas* from Lahori Darwaza and share with her school friends. She talks about the popular Mela Chiraghan (Festival of Lights) and Holi and Diwali, which she would openly participate in, dancing and eating with her Hindu friends. The only restriction was buying miniature sculptures of gods, which her mother had prohibited her from doing. It is during this narration that Kumrud comes up in our conversation.

'She was my classmate—a Hindu girl but also a great friend. We both were very interested in dancing and students and teachers would often ask us to perform for them, which we would, happily putting up a show,' she smiles. 'I remember after I got married and took up dancing as a profession I would often think about her, about our practice. I would wonder where she had gone. And then the most fascinating thing happened. I was asked to come to Karachi for a show and she had been called, too. I had no idea that she had become a big dancer in India and taught her own class! She had brought her students to perform at the show. It was so nice to sit beside her, to judge the young students in front of us. I saw her group performing Kathak from India while she saw mine and we sat for hours afterwards, remembering the school days and the performances we would put up.' Remarkable, I think. Two young girls—even younger than their students today—practised together in their childhood only to grow up to be leading dancers on opposing ends of the border. What had joined them in their youth had brought them together in their adulthood; dance binding Kumrud and Roshan Ara as much as India and Pakistan.

Later, as her college celebrated its fiftieth anniversary, other friends started making their way into Pakistan too and a series of reunions took place. 'Sitting together with these old friends just took us back into those days. We recalled all these stories, each other's little habits, interests. One of my friends, Lalita, reminded me how superstitious I used to be. I wouldn't even let anyone touch my nose!' she leans back shaking with laughter, her mouth covered with her hand, and I cannot help but wonder if she knows how fortunate she is. Roshan Ara is one of the handful people from the Partition generation who has reconnected with friends and neighbours. Her classmates have visited her in Lahore while her profession and family connections have taken her across the border several times. Of course, this hasn't been as easy as it was before Partition but her trips have certainly been frequent enough. Unlike most people, she has been able to reunite with loved ones, she has been able to relive the moments that for many fade away as rusty memories or unfulfilled dreams.

'I spent my honeymoon in India too. This was in 1953. My husband's aunt used to live in Delhi and we went to visit her for a few days before going up to Nainital, this beautiful hill station. But I was too involved in my honeymoon to locate friends on this trip,' she lets out a muffled laugh, red colour washing over her cheeks. 'I didn't go back for some years after that and when I did, I already had a son!' It was about 1957 by this time and Roshan Ara had travelled with her sister and cousins to take full advantage of the Indian market, which sold things that were no longer available in Lahore; they were now 'Indian' items, not to be shared openly with the enemy country. 'We bought so many saris, bundles and bundles of them! I bought a lot of silver jewellery too and we ate many vegetables, went to Chandni Chowk, saw Ramlila at the Ramlila Ground. It was great fun. The shopkeepers bend over backwards when they hear you're from Pakistan. We would be offered drinks, plates of *dahi bhalla, chaat.* They would open the whole shop for us!'

It was during this trip that Roshan Ara decided to trace her old friends. How nice it would be if she could see them just once more, she thought. 'We hadn't kept in contact till then but being in Delhi, I wanted to try and get in touch. Where is so and so, what would they be doing? Of course, I couldn't find everyone. I was just there for a week and would have to wait for the reunion in Lahore to meet most of them but I did find some common friends ... sister's friends, my friends, husband's friends who knew my house in Mussoorie. Any familiar name or place would make us so happy. We would sit and talk about what had happened in our lives.' It was during this trip that Roshan Ara met her closest friends, Kamal Mohini and Saroj, her classmates from school. 'We all met up and talked and talked. They were so nostalgic about Lahore; in fact, anyone who belonged to Lahore was more than nostalgic about it. They would ask us to describe the streets, to tell them what had happened to their homes, where the ice-cream*wala chacha* was. When the Indian director Shyam Benegal and his wife came to Pakistan they stayed with us. His wife, who was from Lahore, also rushed to see her broken house on Waris Road. She even went and located her tailor who used to come to her home and stitch all her clothes. I think it's just not possible to forget Lahore if you've lived here once. It doesn't matter how long ago.'

Roshan Ara is right. People from Lahore have the city stirring in their hearts. The main arteries, the Mall Road and Anarkali, are alive for them. They adore it, they miss it. Lahore for the once-upon-a-time Lahoris is as sacred as Delhi for the *Dilliwalas*. The name of the city, the language of its people, set off a gush of nostalgic feelings, a series of memories, and at times, even tears. I can only imagine how emotional Roshan Ara's friends must have been to talk to her about everything they had left behind in their beloved Lahore. I want to know if her experience of crossing over has been as overwhelming. How have Roshan Ara's journeys been different from before, from visiting or living in Kapurthala, Jaipur and Musoorie before Partition? How has it felt to interact with her childhood friends in *their* country, with them holding a different nationality, an exclusionary citizenship?

'When you're sitting with your friends you don't discuss politics or conflicts. We would catch up on each other's lives, what all had happened in our time away. The antagonism never crept into our conversations. But, of course, it was very different being in India now. Officially, at least, I didn't belong there no matter what your heart or your friends say. On paper, I was a foreigner, a tourist. And I could detect a slight hostility, suspicion among the general public when they heard where you were from. Mind you, that isn't there all the time but it's something that can burst out at any given moment.'

As I jot down notes in my diary, she stops talking for a few seconds and it looks as if she is in deep thought. Then she says, 'I suppose there was some resentment too. I mean, we were happy to have made Pakistan but they felt their country was divided. They had lost out. I remember I once stayed with this Hindu friend of ours and her mother kept talking about how Partition was such a bad thing and it really bothered me because Pakistan is such a big accomplishment for us despite the personal losses we had to bear. My own mother had fought hard for it. But I think I can understand how they feel, they went through exactly what we went through when East Pakistan broke away from us.'

As she says this, I for the first time realize how much India really lost in 1947. Being a Pakistani, I had only ever thought about our losses, the people and homes that had been left behind, the generations-old bonds that were severed. I also saw how it was a gain for Pakistanis like Malik Siddiqui (Chapter Five) and Roshan Ara—a struggle that ended well, a nation built. This perhaps did not lessen the pain of those who had been ripped apart from loved ones, who had lost friends and relatives in the bloodshed, but it was indeed pacifying to know that something so meaningful had been achieved in return.

But for India and its Partition generation, not only had relationships and connections, property and assets, been snatched away, but they had also lost a large chunk of their land, a huge part of their country. This was an immense loss, one which would be difficult to reconcile with. Reading through

Indian history school textbooks, I had noticed a resonance of longing and wistfulness whenever 1947 was discussed. The same topic, which was documented as a momentous victory in Pakistan, evoked a sense of nostalgia in Indian texts. Perhaps, the spin on the same event meant that Indians and Pakistanis had different ways of looking at Partition, of understanding the implications. One's triumph was the other's heartache. No wonder suspicion and mistrust mar our relations even today.

'Whenever we are playing a game or are in competition with the Indians, some of that resentment comes out,' Roshan Ara says after a quiet moment. A leading dancer and bridge player in Pakistan, she has more than once represented Pakistan on international platforms, including in India. 'It gets unpleasant. It becomes more than just about the game. There is a sense of divide now unlike in our childhood. If you beat India you feel superior, you feel happy, and there is this special thrill. And the same goes for them. But despite all that, despite all the grudges we hold, somehow we always end up coming together, especially when we are in another country.' Whenever the Bridge Federation of Asia, Africa and Middle East gets together, Pakistanis and Indians instantly glue, she says. 'We are always the friendliest with each other. After all, we do have so much more in common than we do with, say, Jordan or Egypt, though they are Muslim countries. Most of my memories of these international tours are of eating *chaat* and talking about music with the Indians. There is always this closeness, this magnetic feeling that we share so much.'

It is intriguing to me that while Roshan Ara keeps referring to the Indians she grew up with as 'they' and 'them', a very common attitude found in the majority of Pakistanis today, she cannot also help but assert the intimacy and connection she has with 'them'. She is a cross between the first and second generations of Pakistan. She has grown up amongst Hindus and Sikhs in the undivided subcontinent. There will always be a sense of belonging, of a shared past between her and them. Yet she has also spent the majority of her years in a Pakistan that is opposed to India, a Pakistan that has fought several wars across the border. Her friends now belong to another country, *they* have a distinct nationality. The links between her and her friends may continue to cut through that fine separation but the relationship they hold with each other is not without its complications. While *they* may never become the *other* that they mostly are to the younger generations in Pakistan today, *they* will also always fall short of what they would mean to Naseer Ashiq's (Chapter One) father—who was adopted by a Sikh family—or even to divided families like Shireen's (Chapter Four) or Malik Siddiqui's (Chapter Five) who continue to hold a close relationship across the border—and to Roshan Ara's own mother, who were far older at Partition and had lived for the majority of their lives among Hindus and Sikhs.

Like Roshan Ara, this second generation of Pakistanis—and I assume of Indians too—continues to vacillate between hostility and friendship, between 'home' and 'enemy'. The distinctions aren't clear-cut to them; their association, their recollections not as strong as those of their parents. They have grown up on this side or that. The dissections that are blurred for Naseer Ashiq's father and his Sikh family or even for divided families like Shireen's and Malik Siddiqui are not as hazy for Roshan Ara and many others in her generation. They are Pakistani or Indian. They cannot be both. To make sense of the resentment and love, of bitterness and warmth, is the only confused reality for them.

The glass door opens quietly and Roshan Ara's son walks in. We greet each other and he says sorry before reminding his mother of her appointment. She looks at me apologetically and tells me that she has to be somewhere. I am sad that we cannot speak more and even sadder because she is soon moving to Karachi. After her husband's death, Roshan Ara has been living alone in her house in DHA Society (Defence Housing Authority) in Lahore. Her sons now feel that she should not live on her own. Someone should be around to take care of her. She tells me that she's touched but feels independent enough. For a few years now she has been resisting this move, which will take her away from her love, Lahore. But after months and months of persuasion she has finally given in. Cardboard boxes block half of her entrance. She will be leaving soon.

As she comes to the driveway to see me off, she gives me a hug and thanks me for taking her back into those days that she had put aside in the corners of her memory. We part ways and I'm half-way into my car when she says, 'I really hope you complete this book, that it reaches people. We all, everyone of my age or older, went through a horrible time when Partition happened but we've moved on, we've built our lives on the opposite sides. We must let go of all this animosity too now. India is a wonderful place to visit. It's a familiar place . . . the language, the people, the food. You never feel like you're in an alien land.' I smile and thank her for sharing her experiences and feelings so openly with me. She smiles back and says: 'Do write that Indian movies are my weakness and so are their saris!' I promise her I will and she breaks into another girlish giggle, one that rings in my ears as I make my way home.

chapter seven

AT HOME IN ENEMY COUNTRY

MR AND MRS INTIKHAB ALAM

'Ironically, I was on the last train from Simla to Lahore at Partition, and twenty-four years later, on the last flight to the West Wing before the creation of Bangladesh.' I am sitting with Intikhab Alam, the legendary Pakistani cricketer. Having played countless matches for his country between the 1950s and '70s, Intikhab later began coaching the Pakistan team, playing a part in their victory in the 1992 World Cup and the 2009 Twenty20 World Cup series.

When I first met him, I thought we would speak about cricket, especially the tournaments he played in India. After conversing with Roshan Ara (Chapter Six), I wanted to speak to some more Indian or Pakistani professionals who had worked on either side of the border. I wanted to know about their experiences, their interactions with the 'other'. When a close friend of mine arranged the interview with Intikhab Alam, I was thrilled. I had several questions to ask. How did it feel to represent Pakistan in one of the most hostile states, in

enemy territory? How did a sport as competitive and sacred to
Pakistanis and Indians as cricket translate on to the playing
field? How did he feel being part of a game where triumph or
defeat would come to reflect upon the state of his country, an
authentication of its strength and superiority, or its reverse?

Yet in the hours I spent sitting with Intikhab in his house
in Model Town, the topic of cricket took up no more than two
or three minutes. Within seconds of our introduction, I came
to realize that India was not just a place to play cricket, an
enemy meant to be defeated. Rather it was home for Intikhab.
As for Roshan Ara (Chapter Six), it was a home of the past;
one that could not deny him his childhood memories and
heritage.

'My father was an engineer, actually,' he starts. 'He was
heading the electricity department in Simla in 1947. I was
about five years old at this time.' He sucks in air, holding his
breath before continuing. 'When it all started . . . things became
. . . extremely hard because we were the only Muslim family in
Simla at that time. A lot of people had left.' I am surprised to
see the difficulty with which Intikhab is speaking. The pauses,
the heavy breathing, is unexpected. He has been interviewed
by numerous domestic and international media channels in
the past. This is just another interview, and that too an informal
one set up by his son's friend's friend. But perhaps it's the first
time someone has asked Intikhab to speak not about his
career or his success but rather about his past, about Partition.

'My father was a government servant.' His voice comes out
weak, barely audible, and I have to move closer to the edge of
the sofa to hear him better. 'He was in charge of the whole
electricity department, so we couldn't leave in time. We
thought we would really be okay . . . until the trouble started.'

As riots escalated, the Khan family became scared that they were at risk inside their own four walls and quickly scrambled into their Sikh neighbour's home. 'He was my father's number two, an incredibly loyal fellow,' explains Intikhab. 'He came to my father one day and said: "Khan sahib you have to leave your house. Things have become very, very difficult. They won't leave you alive."

'For the next three days we stayed cooped up in a small room with the Sikh family, without a clue about our future. The mob used to come and the Sikh would tell them that the Khan family had already left. They came three-four times but he continued to safeguard us till he could.'

However, as violence seeped into Simla, leaving blood and scars at every crossing and alley, Khan's neighbour began to fear for his life as much as theirs. 'One night he came and said, "It's become very difficult to protect you. They want to search my house, you have to leave or they'll kill all of us." I think it was one or twelve o'clock when he said leave, leave now.' The Sikh, whose name Intikhab doesn't mention, grabbed a torch and paved his way through the jungle, guiding the Khan family to the power house responsible for generating electricity. He wanted to make sure that they would be safe. 'It took us about an hour or so to go down through the jungle to the power house and he stayed with us the whole time. I don't know if we would have made it without his help. I still remember when we first heard the tremendous sound of the engines producing electricity my father and he flung into each other's arms. We all couldn't believe we had made it there.'

This was not the first time I was hearing of opposite sides coming to the rescue. Intikhab's family was being saved by their Sikh neighbour in the middle of Muslim-Sikh tensions.

Many people I had spoken to had narrated similar instances of compassion and support offered by the 'other', whether Muslim, Hindu or Sikh. In some of the recent literature on 1947, which includes Yasmin Khan's *The Great Partition* and Rajmohan Gandhi's *Punjab: A History from Aurangzeb to Mountbatten*, such 'rescue' stories have also been documented as a window into the humanity that prevailed during the chaos of Partition. Ashis Nandy's work on Partition reveals similar findings. In conducting 1500 interviews, he found that '40 per cent of his sample called up stories of themselves and others being helped through the orgy of blood and death by somebody from the other side'.[6] I had also heard that many a time people who belonged to the religious clergy of their respective faiths, that is, pandits and maulvis, also came to the rescue of the opposite communities.

I had been surprised when I first came across such stories; I had conveniently assumed for the majority of my years that all Muslims, Sikhs and Hindus were at each other's throats, and especially those who had religious affiliations. At most a handful may have tried to help the 'other' but to me such stories never really seemed relevant enough to explore; I assumed that even if they were true, they were mere exceptional cases. However, increasingly, I was finding out that I had been wrong.

Intikhab tells me that that was the last time his family saw their Sikh saviour. His father's Muslim friend, a brigadier, was going to help them from there on. As part of this rescue mission, the brigadier asked the family if they wanted to collect

[6]Nandy, Ashis, *Pakistan's latent 'potentialities'*, Radio Open Source. Web: http://radioopensource.org/ashis-nandy-on-pakistans-latent-potentialities/ (Last accessed: 24 November 2014).

anything from their house before being transported to their new home, somewhere in the newly-formed state of Pakistan. To the five-year-old Intikhab, all of this did not make much sense. Religion? Hindu-Muslim divide? New home? Pakistan was just a word which used some of the new ABC alphabets he had recently learnt. It was P-A-K-I-S-T-A-N, a simple yet proud addition to his vocabulary. 'I still remember that as we waited in the truck, my mother went inside the house and brought back the Quran and whatever cash and jewellery we had. And that was it,' he snaps his fingers, 'with that, we just left our packed house and made our way forward to Ladakhi Mohalla, where my father knew a few people, and then to Kalka.'

'At Kalka, it was an open field without any shelter or anything. There were stones and garbage scattered everywhere. We spent two nights there in those conditions. I remember in the evenings they would fire and bullets would fly through our tent, which we had made out of sticks and my mother's *dupattas*.'

'Who were *they*?' I interrupt. 'Sikhs,' he replies in a matter-of-fact way. They would fire everywhere at random,' he pauses and twirls his hand in the air for a moment and then looks at me. 'At one end we were being helped by the Sikhs and at the other end they were attacking us. There was absolutely no logic.'

As he says this I realize how easy it is to believe that all Hindus and Sikhs were bad. Had Intikhab not narrated the story of his father's Sikh neighbour to me, the notion of 'big bad Sikhs' I had come across in my school textbooks—which I will discuss at length later—and in news bulletins and in general discussions among people while growing up in Pakistan, would only have been reinforced. But as I hear his story, the flip side of the coin, I realize how naïve it is to characterize a group of people as entirely good or bad, or a situation as complex as Partition as black or white. The conditions were far more complicated, far more twisted than presented in our official accounts of history. How could I have believed at a point in my life that all Sikhs and Hindus had turned evil overnight and all Muslims were pure? As I shake my head at my ignorance, Intikhab's voice draws me back into the room.

'From Kalka, we boarded a train but the situation was even worse inside. Sikhs were searching trains to see if anyone was a government servant and we knew that if they saw our father, they would kill each one of us. This was after Partition and by this time a Muslim, and especially an official, caught in what was now Indian territory, often had only one destiny—torture before death. The drivers would park the train in the jungle and then honk to alert the Sikhs to come kill everyone aboard. It was an open invitation.'

Intikhab leans backward, his chest broad against the sofa he is sitting on. His body is charged, his face alert after a long day of work. He isn't narrating an adventure story; this was reality for him. All without any rationale for the five-year-old Intikhab or the over-sixty-year-old Khan. 'That day there were two trains. *Ghalti se*—by mistake—they, the Sikhs, got the information that the first one was a goods train. The driver parked the train in the middle of a jungle and we stayed there for over three hours. The driver kept honking but no one came to inquire, to kill, and the train eventually moved forward to Pakistan. At the next train they shot and shot but there was no one inside. That's how we survived.'

We stop conversing momentarily as Mrs Alam walks in with grape juice and dry fruit. We introduce ourselves and she takes a corner seat in the room. I turn towards Intikhab once again and ask him if he remembers how he felt about leaving his home, about everything he had witnessed? I had found that people narrating Partition stories or, for that matter, even incidents about the 1965 or 1971 war, often gave detailed and elaborate accounts of what they had experienced even if they had been very young at the time—it always astonished me that they could have absorbed so much at such a young age. Perhaps it is the traumatic nature of such events; it has a way of sensitizing, of maturing even children. Or perhaps, the young survivors had internalized the stories they had heard from their parents, the experiences of their elders had become their own reality.

'I was very very quiet. *Dekh raha tha ke kya katlo gharat ho rahi hai. Aam log massacre ho rahe hain. Auratein mari hoey hein. Kisi ka sar gayab hai tou kisi ke paer.* (I was looking around at the bloodshed, at the massacre of common people. Women were lying dead, some with their heads missing, some without legs.) I remember standing at the railway station, thirsty for a drink of water, which cost a hundred rupees. Even people's monthly salary wasn't as much. Today, whenever I speak to the young boys in the cricket team, I tell them how hard we fought for Pakistan. They cannot even begin to imagine the kind of sacrifices we made for this country. *Abhi bhi mein un kuti hoey aurton, mardon, bachon ke barey mein sochta hoon tou meri ajeeb halat ho jati hai.* (Even today when I think about those chopped-up bodies of men, women and children, I feel ill.)'

I can almost taste dry blood in my throat as he recalls the scene, creating a vivid picture for me. Pools of blood, headless bodies, breasts cut up. It is almost as if I can see them too. Just then his wife, Mahe Darakhshaan, speaks up from the corner.

'Seven men from my family were martyred during Partition. The women, meanwhile, jumped into the wells.' Silence follows. She says nothing more and I don't know how to respond.

Movies like *Khamosh Pani* have depicted horrid scenes of women choosing, or being forced by family members, to drown themselves due to the fear of being abducted or raped by Muslims or non-Muslims—depending on which religion they belonged to. Another gentleman from the Partition generation I had spoken to once had told me, 'We were from a very conservative Muslim family. Even when our women had to go out to the markets, a special time was allotted during which all the men in the village would go inside their houses, and only then would the women be allowed outside. They simply could not be seen. When at Partition we were informed that we must migrate to save our lives, we just did not know what to do with the women. We could certainly not make them travel with us. They had never left their homes to travel such a distance! The only option was to throw them in the wells. This was to protect them more than anything else. I took my own sisters to the well to do the same but at the last minute I stopped. Something in me snapped and I realized I couldn't drown them with my own bare hands.'

Swallowing uncomfortably, I look at Mrs Alam. 'Your family was from India too?'

'Yes, our families lived side by side in Hoshiarpur where my husband was born,' she looks at Intikhab before continuing. 'There were two villages, one small and one big. They were called *joron di basti* because apart from their size, they were identical to each other. Even though I was born after Partition in Pakistan, most of my childhood and even adulthood was spent listening to my parents' stories from there.'

I'm happy to see that Mrs Alam is willing to talk, and ask her to tell me more about her family, about these stories. 'My mother was from Hoshiarpur, my father from Jalandhar. At the time of Partition she had been married off in Jalandhar. That was the only reason she survived. She lost her mother, her two brothers, their wives, their six children and three servants, all of whom were still in the *joron di basti* in Hoshiarpur. Only she and two of my uncles who had settled abroad survived and reached Pakistan.'

The list of the lost ones rolls off her tongue with a strange ease. It's a reality she has grown up with, one that I assume would have shaped how she sees her family's past, how she looks at Partition and currently, the 'other' on the opposite side of the border. She echoes my thoughts when a moment later she says, '*Bachpan mein*—in my childhood—I was really scared of Sikhs and Hindus. I had heard such terrible stories. I thought they were horrible people. This was the case until I went to Europe and lived beside them. It was only then that I realized they weren't villains, that they were humans like us.' Her experience seems to resonate entirely with my own. Hindus and Sikhs were mischief-makers and infidels, I had thought, until I had actually interacted with them, sitting far away in Canada. Their transformation from evil-doers to ordinary people had been a slow U-turn from my childhood perceptions.

'On the other hand, the stories I grew up hearing made me look at Pakistan in a different way too. *Iski betahasha qadar thee* (we really cared for our country). We had lost so much for it, how could we not value it?' Mrs Alam adds.

I nod in agreement. There is a strong nationalist fervour burning in sections of the youth even today. We have all grown up listening to similar struggles of our grandparents, about how much they sacrificed for this country. Yet many are in a race to get their green cards and work permits, anxious to leave behind the political unrest, the crippled economy, the bomb blasts and security threats. But listening to such traumatic experiences forces me to rethink what Pakistan really means to some of us Pakistanis. To Mrs Alam the brutal death of several family members is the price of her homeland. To Malik Siddiqui (Chapter Five) the permanent distance between him and his loved ones is the cost of Pakistan. For Shireen's (Chapter Four) mother, the constant ache of being ripped away from her Bombay, is the pain she had to bear for this land. To these people, what does Pakistan mean? I can probably never begin to understand or value it like them. And I am probably not the only one . . .

'I didn't see all that Intikhab did. As I said, I was born after Partition, here in Pakistan. But I had heard so much that by the time I went there, I already had a clear image of Hoshiarpur and my mother's home.' You were able to go see it? I ask. 'Yes, when I went to India—I think this was in 1982—I went to see my place of origin. I didn't just want to listen to the stories anymore; I wanted to see it with my own eyes, and it felt really good. My mother's house was just the same as she had told me; the same windows, doors, the same big house in the middle of the fields, the same huge mango trees surrounding it at every corner. A few Sikhs were living there but they still hadn't removed the *ayats* my family had inscribed on the walls years ago.'

I ask her how her mother felt about her going back and

notice that the tip of her nose has turned a deep shade of pink. Her eyes are watery and her voice thick. 'My mom, even my uncles, they were all so excited because until then no one had travelled back. My grandfather is buried in front of the house in Hoshiarpur and I was the first one who was able to read *Surah Al-Fatiha* there. I had never imagined that I would be able to offer my prayers at his grave ... When I told my mother this, she was very emotional. She was happy that at least someone had visited the house after so many years. We used to read *Fatiha* here but it's not the same thing. Being at the grave, and seeing how the locals had respected it ... it was such a beautiful feeling.'

I cannot help but think how strange it is that Mrs Alam's mother, who had lost almost her entire family at Partition, had wanted her daughter to go back. My grandmother, who was born and brought up in what later became Pakistan and who had seen the terrible conditions the refugees arrived in in Lahore, had more than often told me never to go to India. When I did go, she uttered a hushed '*tobah tobah*'. She told me Hindus were like snakes, mischievous and treacherous; that they had taken away everything from Muslims. She felt that I was dishonouring our history by wanting to travel across, to learn about our neighbour, to make friends. As a child, I had understood why she felt this way; after all the bloodshed she had seen, I could make sense of the hatred she felt for those who she held responsible. But hearing Mrs Alam, I question why my grandmother felt so much animosity and such a strong desire to distance herself from India when she had, fortunately, not lost a single family member to Partition? How was Mrs Alam's mother able to ask her daughter to go visit, to go back to that past despite everything she had suffered? Was it because she had lived in that land for too long? That she couldn't reject that past, as bloody as it was? That it was her heritage, one she couldn't separate herself from despite living miles away for so many years? That she had too much on that side to let go, to distance herself from, including her father's grave? Was it easier for my grandmother to cut off because she never had to leave her home, because she didn't have to leave family members buried or alive on the other side? That it thus became easier to just let go of what became Indian territory as one which inhabited the evil 'other'? Did the experiences and understanding of the migrant communities vary drastically from those who became hosts to the refugees? This was probably another topic of research on its own, one that I would have to explore at another point in life.

'I went back too, to see one of my homes,' Intikhab speaks suddenly, his voice emotionally charged. My thoughts are interrupted and I turn towards him. 'We had two homes . . . in Simla, where we left everything, and one in Hoshiarpur, where I was born. I was in India, in fact, in Jalandhar, where I was playing a match for Pakistan, when I had a chance to go see my birth place. I remembered that house too. It was in a hilly area and every winter we would go there and in the summers come back to Simla. It had a huge wooden gate, besides which there was a tubewell which was our own. There was a kitchen inside and three bedrooms, with a staircase taking you to the rooftop. In front of our house there was a small plot where we used to play as children. Our house was in the *basti*, about forty-five minutes away from Hoshiarpur. We would have to sit on a horse or *bailgaadi* to go to the town because there was no other way of transport. Everyone would walk a lot, even the women and children, and we would have to travel through a *choh*—a canal full of sand—which would overflow whenever it rained. When my wife and I went to see my house the *choh* was still there. The only difference was that we could drive through it this time.'

When Mr and Mrs Alam reached the *basti*, they were taken aback. The house was just as Intikhab remembered. The same wooden gate, the same tubewell stood to receive him. 'Nothing had changed. No renovations had been done. Even the road names were the same! Just the *mombattis* and *diyas* (candles) had been replaced with electricity and telephone lines. The family that lived there had also made a small *mandir* in the house but some of the *ayats* of the Holy Quran were still engraved on the walls. It was shocking to see how similar everything was all these years later.'

He moves forward and raises his hands midway, his palms facing me, before continuing, 'You won't believe it but when we entered the house, a man who must have been about eighty or eighty-five years old was painting the walls and asking the family, "*Aap ko pata hai aap se pehle idhar kaun log rahte thai? Yahan Khan sahib ki family rehti thi.*" (Khan sahib's family used to live here before Partition.) When we told him who we were he almost fell off his ladder in shock! He couldn't believe it.' Intikhab relaxes back in the chair and I notice that the anxiousness, the nervousness with which he recalled the Partition days have disappeared. He is happy to speak about his travels to his ancestral home.

'We even met some people my mother had told me about. They were stunned to hear who I was. A few of them began to cry and asked me where my family had suddenly vanished.

They opened their homes to us and showered us with milk and sweets. They even made me drink water from the tubewell in front of my house!' He lets out a long sigh and says, 'I've been to Hoshiarpur two-three times since then and it always feels good to be there. There are three Sikh families living there now but they are exceptionally warm and hospitable each time.'

I ask Intikhab if he has been as fortunate about locating his home in Simla. 'Well, yes and no,' he answers. 'I had taken the Punjab cricket team over to India for a match. I thought they should get some time off before playing, to relax and see more of India, so I decided to take them to Simla, many years after my family had left it.' Nostalgia creeps into his voice as he tells me about this journey; the pain from an old wound, a loss, is visible. 'I knew the address of my house, 2 Kot Hill, and I told everyone I wanted to go see my home and set out one day to locate it.'

Intikhab was confident that he would find his home intact, just as in Hoshiarpur. But once he reached Kot Hill after hours of tedious searching, his house was nowhere to be found. '*Kot Hill milla tou woh ghar hi nahi milla* (I found Kot Hill but I couldn't find my home). It was a beautiful house. I remember, from the dining room you could see the entire jungle, all the fruit trees. The viceroy's headquarters was nearby and he used to spend his summer vacations over there as well. I searched and searched but couldn't see my house. The whole area had become a jungle. I don't know if my house was demolished or what but I suppose at least I should be thankful that I saw Kot Hill once more. No one else in my family has been able to do so and I have.'

Intikhab's next step was the Kalka train station, from where the family had boarded the train on that overwhelming and life-threatening day over six decades ago. He tells me that the station looked just the same, reviving his memories of the bloodshed of Partition. But thankfully, the visit did have its brighter side. As he crossed the station, Intikhab came across several of his father's old friends and neighbours who had settled in Simla. 'They still remembered my family, that we'd spent our summers over there. Meeting them again, seeing my home again, has made me peaceful. There was this anxiety in me that has been silenced.'

Hearing his story, I assume that for Intikhab, who has grown up in the same Pakistan that Roshan Ara (Chapter Six) has—a Pakistan that is adverse to India—his relationship with the 'other', like hers, is more complicated than it is for most Pakistanis. Most of his memories are soaked in his parents' tender recollections. He is also one of the only ones from his family who has been able to go back to see his home, to acknowledge his heritage on the other side. He has been welcomed over and over again. He himself recalls how his Sikh neighbour rescued his family; he can see how warmly his father's friends receive him even now. But at the same time, Intikhab has a present which is only rooted in Lahore, in the divided subcontinent. India is the archrival, the enemy neighbour that Pakistan spends enormous amounts of money to defend itself against. I assume this must have some impact on his relationship with India. I ask him to tell me how he makes sense between his past and his present, between friend and foe. He takes a few seconds to respond.

'*Dekho betey India ke saath bara ajeeb rishta hai. Woh ghar bhi hai, dushman bhi hai.* (Look, daughter, my relationship with India is rather strange. It is home and yet it is also the enemy country.) But I think too much time has gone by to remember all that went wrong. I mean I've even lived there for two years and they looked after me so well. I made friends, I went to my home. What more could I want?'

To call India a home of the past is okay, it is legitimized because of our shared history. For the Partition generation to refer to it as their home is perhaps somewhat acceptable as well. Most of them had spent the majority of their lives there. But for someone like Intikhab, who was nurtured on this side of the border, who had grown up to represent Pakistan and take her ownership around the world, such a statement could be construed as unpatriotic. Hesitatingly, I ask him if he still sees India as home and I'm received with silence, making me wonder if I should have refrained from such a question. Had I offended him? Had I touched a sensitive patriotic nerve? I am thinking of how to retract my words carefully when he speaks again.

'I don't know what to say. I would say it is just a dream. So much happened to my family at Partition and yet we got out alive, we built our lives and moved on. And today I can go back. I can speak Punjabi with them, I can drink water from our tubewell, I can stand in the room I was born in. I don't know what to call that feeling. Is it still my home? Can it still be my home? I don't know. All I know is that each time I'm there it feels like a dream.'

It is indeed a dream, I tell him, one that few have had the luxury of dreaming. Just a day before I had been told that Muhammad Rauf (Chapter Two) from Sahiwal, the man who had pushed me to write this book, had passed away; he had suffered a major heart attack. His longing to see his home once more had died with them. The few minutes he had spent in his birthplace, through the bus window, or by standing at the border, were going to be his only reunification with his home. Many across India and Pakistan would not even get this opportunity. But at least in this house, in the Alam family, there is some closure, some sense of belonging. Someone has been able to pray at the grave of a loved one; someone has been able to meet those he had left behind. Someone has been able to set foot in his home again.

chapter eight

A DAUGHTER FULFILS HER MOTHER'S DYING WISH

AMBREEN RAJA

I came across Ambreen Raja through one of my colleagues, Maria. 'She recently went to India to see her parents' home. You should speak with her.' I was excited about talking to Ambreen for two reasons. First, I desperately wanted to know more about the experiences of Pakistanis exploring their heritage. Ambreen, I was told, was born in Pakistan in 1962—much after Partition. I wanted to know whether her India experience was different from that of Partition survivors like Intikhab Alam (Chapter Seven) and Roshan Ara (Chapter Six). And second, I wanted to meet her because she was the wife of Ramiz Raja, the former batsman and captain of the Pakistan cricket team and currently, a commentator across the border.

In a country where people breathe, eat and sleep cricket, I wouldn't dare to consider myself an ardent follower of the sport. I am more likely one of those who watch the cricket World Cup every four years, strongly supporting the green team without much knowledge of any of the fresh faces on the field. Yet I consider myself a fan. In Pakistan, it is rather difficult to not have some sort of association or following of cricket. The country is conflict-ridden, factionalized, parched for a sense of identity and belonging even sixty-seven years after its creation. Cricket serves to be that one factor that unifies: the children and the adults, the 'conservative' and the 'modern', the cities and the villages. The cricket season is the one time when the poor and the rich stand together, craning their necks to gain a glimpse of the game, praying with all their might for their country. After all, Pakistan really could use some positive coverage in the international media. Cricket is the sport that brings out the patriotic in even the most unpatriotic.

As Ambreen and I begin to talk, she tells me that she visited India for the 2005 India-Pakistan cricket series. Cricket between the two countries would come to an abrupt halt after the 2008 Mumbai attacks. In her words, 'Like our political relations, our cricket relations are also very fickle. In 2004 our relations had become okay after about ten years or so. The Indian team had come to Pakistan to play and in 2005 it was our turn. The deal was that the teams would alternate and come every year but then 2008 happened.'

Cricket has been seen by many, including policymakers and top-level advisors, as a diplomatic tool to bring peace between the two countries. India is no less cricket crazy than Pakistan and a match between the two antagonistic states brings both nations to a standstill. I saw the India-Pakistan T-20 World Cup match in Delhi on my last visit in late 2012. I was in Lajpat Nagar, shopping for Indian *khussas* (traditional shoes) about an hour before the match was to begin. Every little shop in the crowded market had the sports channel playing. As I asked the shopkeeper to show me something unique he distractedly looked away from the commentary and pointed to bright pink *khussas*, 'Madam, that one is specially from Pakistan, you won't find it anywhere else.' I laughed and said, '*Aye hai*, please, I don't want another Pakistani shoe.' As he snickered, I realized he probably saw me as an anti-Pakistan Indian buyer, not realizing that I was from Pakistan and the last thing I wanted was more Pakistani-styled shoes. He returned to his commentary and shouted to the nearby shopkeepers, '*Oye match shuru hone wala hai, chai le aao, Pakistan humare haath dhulney wala hai.*' (Bring some tea, Pakistan's about to lose big time.)

Later, as I watched the match crammed in between hundreds of Indian fans at the Select City Mall in Saket, I couldn't help but recall the shopkeeper and how right he had been. Pakistan lost horribly and each blow to the team hit me hard as I heard screams and euphoria resonate through the mall. I couldn't help but shriek at the fall of every wicket and managed to get the stares of many charged young men around me. I was one of the only girls right at the front and perhaps that was the moment that I felt my Pakistani identity burn in me the most. I had never felt myself to be in such a minority. The friends who I was with were also Indian, laughing and slapping my back each time the green team made another mistake. My only Pakistani male colleague yelled out '*Jai Hind*', with the rest of the crowd. Upon my glares he sheepishly responded, 'You're a girl! If I cheer for Pakistan here, I'll be black and blue in two minutes!' He was probably right. Cricket is no joke for India and Pakistan. Often the losing side begins to set things on fire or turns violent in the stadium. The victory or failure of a team in an India-Pakistan cricket match goes well beyond a game for most of the audience. It stands as a testimony to the overall state of the winning and losing parties, not as teams but as nations, marred with lines of abhorrence, bloodshed and animosity.

I ask Ambreen about her early experiences of such matches between India and Pakistan but she says she doesn't have any. 'To tell you the truth, I was always the superstitious kind so when Ramiz was playing in the team, I would never attend the matches. I was afraid that my sitting in the audience would bring some kind of bad luck to him and the team would lose,' she answers shyly, 'It was only when he joined the Pakistan cricket board that I started to go along with him to the matches. One of the first places I accompanied him to was India.'

India was a country that Ambreen had been running away from for many years. It was the birthplace of both her parents, a country where her mother and father had spent much of their childhood, a nation which had united them in the everlasting bond of marriage. 'My father's name was Afzal Zaidi and my mother was Saghira Begum. He belonged to the Shia sect of Islam while my mother was a Sunni Muslim and under normal circumstances, they would never have got married.'

At the time of Partition, when Hindu, Muslim and Sikh communities stood ravaged, the identities of sub-factions and sects were blurred, and traditional expectations were sidelined. After all, it was much better to marry a fellow Muslim, in or out of family, Sunni or Shia, than to be abducted, raped or married off to a *kafir* (infidel).

'It was April 1947 and Shia-Sunni marriages weren't allowed at that time too. But due to the rioting, Hindus were abducting

Muslim women and so the families got them married off. They were family friends. The *nikaah* was in India on the 4th of April and the *ruksati* in Pakistan, when they moved here after Partition. As children we would tease them that theirs was a marriage of convenience.' Ambreen laughs, her voice thin, on the verge of breaking. Both her parents died in 1999, within ten months of each other. As one of their favourite children, it is a loss that continues to weigh her down. The way she speaks about her parents—fondly, nostalgically—brings a strange life to her. It is as if she is close to crying, but not in sorrow, rather in the warm remembrance of her two idols and the fulfilling years spent with them.

'My father was from Shahbad in east Punjab, near Ambala, and my mother was from Chandni Chowk in Delhi. It was *androon Dilli* (Old Delhi) just like our *androon* Lahore. They both missed their homes terribly but never had a chance to go back.' Late at night after dinner, her parents would recall their days in India. They would remember their time there as peaceful and serene; the society regimented and structured under the British Raj. Ambreen recalls her mother telling her of the evenings when the British would ride on their horses to light the oil lamps in the absence of electricity. 'People would gather around to see them but no one dared to point,' she would say. When Ramiz would return after playing cricket in India, her mother would sit him by her side and ask him to tell her more about Delhi. She wanted to picture the streets, the people and the smells of her beloved city, the lanes where she had grown up, the house where she had matured from a young child to a bride. For years, in fact, just about up to her death, Saghira Begum longed to go back to Delhi. She still remembered it as the pre-Partition state, the *Dilli* of the

Dilliwalas, which had kept her heart strongly clenched within it as she departed for Pakistan, the foreign land which was to become her home.

'As a young child I didn't know why these places were so important to my parents. I had never seen them; I couldn't associate myself with Shahbad or Delhi. I had grown up in Lahore, that was my home,' she sighs. 'And by the time I really began to understand what they meant to my parents, I had already lost them. After that I just wanted to block India out. It reminded me too much of them and that was very painful.'

It was only after many deliberately missed chances that Ambreen finally decided to visit India in 2005. 'Cricket relations had improved after years and everyone was very excited. I thought it was time I went too.' Travelling with a group of people, Ambreen crossed over the Wagah border on foot. Here, the group was given a grand welcome, with the *dhol* playing dramatic music as they stepped across. 'There were many stalls and food dishes set up for us; it was so overwhelming that it sidetracked me from the actual crossing-over experience. People around us were in a frenzy to get Ramiz's autographs and to take pictures with us. It preoccupied me so much that I didn't realize I was going to my parents' birthplace.'

From the border, the group embarked on a journey to Chandigarh. As they drove through the different villages, Ambreen could not help but draw comparisons. 'It was just like driving through a Pakistani village. There were *doodhwalas* carrying *matkas* on each side while the women were working in the fields. The walls were full of the same advertisements, graffiti about *hakeems* and posters of Kareena Kapoor and Shahrukh Khan. The only difference was the Gurmukhi script and the helmet-wearing women riding Hondas—and, of course, the gurdwaras and temples that would crop up.'

The group's first stop was the Golden Temple or the Harmandir Sahib of Amritsar, the most sacred gurdwara for the Sikh community and the most popular tourist site in the city. 'Here we saw the Guru Granth Sahib and the flying whisk. We also had *halwa* as part of what they call *prasad.* It was a beautiful gurdwara.' Ambreen remembers something and lets out a chuckle, 'You know the cricket craze in India is just as bad as Pakistan. We had covered our heads before entering just as you do in a mosque and had taken our shoes off. While doing so, someone recognized Ramiz and stole our shoes! He was a fan but he left us both shoeless! We had to walk barefoot for a while before someone got them back for us.'

As she speaks about her journey, I ask Ambreen how she felt about entering a nation she had so desperately tried to avoid all these years. How was she received by the Indians? What did she think of the places and people she never wanted to see for fear of how it would make her miss her parents? She takes a moment before responding. 'You know, one day I was with Ramiz at his post-match commentary in Mohali. I was sitting outside when a girl from Sahara Channel approached me and asked about my experience. She too wanted to know what I thought of India and the Indians, our so-called enemies. I told her that as Ramiz's wife I could not answer because my experience was very different from that of the common people. As far as I know, they treated me wonderfully. There was no hostility, no discrimination. But later I realized that wasn't true. I may have been treated well because of Ramiz but even otherwise I saw so much love, so much friendship.

'Once I went to Sector 17 in Chandigarh, it's just like our Liberty Market in Lahore. I was with Indian friends so they had no way of telling me apart but my *shalwar* gave me away. It was 2005 and straight *shalwars* were in fashion in Pakistan but in Indian Punjab they were wearing the *gharey wali* (loose) *shalwars*. Once they recognized me they were so hospitable! They offered me sweets, cold drinks, *chaat* over and over again. They even told me "*aap ka rang saaf hai*" (you have a fair complexion), and gave me a 10 per cent discount on everything!' She laughs but then her expression turns sombre, '*Mujhe dukh hota hai*—I feel so sad—when I see the two countries fight. There is so much we can share and I think the common people know that.' Once, when Ambreen was buying groceries, she showed her surprise at the price of tomatoes, which were one-fourth the price in Pakistan. Seeing her reaction, the shopkeeper at the vegetable market said, 'Wouldn't it be so good if we could trade? Take back ten or fifteen kilos with you. The price there is Rs 120 while we sell it for Rs 15-30 here. Imagine the kind of profit!'

But Ambreen's trips to India have not just been about the future possibilities and current relations between the two countries. She has a past in India to explore, one that she couldn't stay away from for too long. 'I had mentioned to the reporter from Sahara TV that my mother was from Delhi and she promised to take me around. At first I was scared. I didn't know if I wanted to go there . . . I couldn't imagine Chandni Chowk without my mother. I didn't want to see it without her.' But when the reporter insisted Ambreen realized that this was her chance to do something for her late mother, who had died without being able to fulfil her wish to see Delhi again.

As she walked through the packed lanes of Old Delhi, places she had heard about from her mother started to materialize. 'I saw Golcha Cinema where my *mamu* (uncle) and mother used to watch movies and walked around Darya Ganj, where my mother had lived. It was so emotional for me that I began to cry.' Ambreen's resolve breaks and she begins to weep silently. 'I felt like my mother was standing there, showing me all the places that had stood so close to her heart. I wish she was still alive and could come here herself. I wish I could've brought her or at least told her that I had finally seen what she had spoken so fondly about.'

When Ramiz returned to India in 2007, Ambreen for the first time insisted that he take her along. This time she wanted to bring her younger sister with her too. She wanted her to experience her emotions as well, to have the same closure; she wanted them both to fulfil their mother's dying wish of going to her birthplace. 'I had always thought Chandni Chowk was a posh area but it is no different from our crowded Anarkali in Lahore. My mother used to get her *dupattas* dyed from there and would tell us about the cycle-rickshaws driven by men. I sat in one and felt like I had gone back in time.' (What one commonly refers to as rickshaws in Pakistan are called autos across the border while cycle-rickshaws are hardly seen in the country.) 'I also saw the Ramlila Ground where my mother said fairs and *melas* would take place and even went to Qutub Minar, Dilli Darwaza and Jama Masjid; my *nana* (maternal grandfather) used to offer his prayers there before Partition. *Ami* had told me about all these places. She would say, "Thank God for memories, for being able to remember my *Dilli*... it is the only thing that gets me by."'

Unfortunately, Ambreen didn't have the exact address of her mother's residence and even if she did, she thought visiting it would be too overwhelming. But by walking along the same streets as her mother had once, Ambreen felt an instant connection. 'There was a bond. I felt at home. My friends even offered to find the house but I just didn't have the time and I was already too emotional. For days afterwards, I couldn't talk to anyone. I was lost in my mom's world.' Bits and pieces of conversations with her parents would creep in and subsume Ambreen for hours. 'I would remember the way my mother spoke about celebrating Holi, Diwali and Eid with her Hindu friends. My father was from Punjab and so he had many Sikh friends. They would tell me that there used to be no stark Hindu-Sikh-Muslim distinction as there is today, that there was a coexistence, even a codependence on each other. Of course, there were communal issues even then but Hindus and Sikhs continued to be their friends both before and after Partition. It was difficult for me to understand this as a child. We were taught differently in schools, where there were no Hindus or Sikhs to be friends with anyway. But for my parents these were some of their closest people. They could never forget them.'

When Sikh pilgrims from India would pour into Pakistan for religious festivals, many of Ambreen's father's friends would come visit them. 'One of them was *Abba's* oldest neighbour. They were like brothers and he would come to our house almost every year. He made it a point to stop over on the way back from Nankana Sahib and have food with us each time. When my father died, he was one of the first people I called. He was terribly sad and up until 2008 I used to speak with him regularly. Sadly, after that I got so busy with my children that we lost touch.' Ambreen tells me that her father and he were so close that they would regularly write letters to each other and never failed to wish one another, whether it was New Year's, Eid or Diwali. When Ambreen first visited India in 2005, years after her father's death, she was able to meet his closest friend one last time.

'The pictures the reporters had taken at the border had been published in the local newspaper. My father's friend saw them and came all the way to Mohali to meet us but the guards wouldn't allow him inside the stadium. He then called Pakistan to get our number and called me. I couldn't believe it when I heard his voice. I rushed out and hugged him . . . I can't tell you what it felt like. I missed my father so much that day.' Afzal Zaidi's childhood friend had put everything aside to meet his neighbour's daughter. Showering her with presents, he sat with her for hours talking about her father and the time they spent together in Shahbad. The links he had with the Zaidi family had survived Afzal's death. The bond was still strong. 'They wanted us to visit their house too but we were on just a five-day visit. I wish I could've gone but it wasn't possible. That was the last time I met him.'

It was when Ramiz saw how emotional his wife was after meeting her father's friend that he decided to take Ambreen to Shahbad where Afzal had grown up. She had seen her mother's city. It was now time to see her father's. 'Shahbad isn't on the way from Mohali to Wagah so we had to take a special route. I remember as we inched closer I saw signboards which read Shahbad. Just seeing the name that I had heard over and over again in my childhood made me realize how close I was to my father's home. His entire childhood had been spent there and I kept thinking, he must have played there, gone to school there. I can't even explain what I felt. I had goosebumps all over; even talking about it now gives me goosebumps.'

Ambreen had been indifferent about her heritage for much

of her childhood. Delhi and Shahbad had held no importance
in her life. But as she lost her parents, the places which were
closest to them started to hold an exceptional meaning for
her. She wanted to explore her roots, she wanted to travel back
to where her mother and father couldn't. She wanted to
complete their journeys for them. But this process has been so
painful that she has created her own boundaries and limitations
in doing so; she has been scared of digging too deep. With
Ramiz's connections and her friends across India, she could
have been one of the few lucky ones who could locate the exact
homes, the correct *mohallas* of their parents. But this is too
difficult for her. Just standing in Darya Ganj and Shahbad is
overwhelming enough; going closer hurts too much. She tells
me that whenever she returned to India between 2005 and
2008, she would always make it a point to drive through
Shahbad and Delhi but she never tried exploring any further.
Ramiz wouldn't let her either.

'He said I got too sentimental afterwards and he was right.
For days I couldn't get out of that mind frame. I still insisted
that we drive through the cities, if nothing else, but I didn't
push for more. Just being in Shahbad and Delhi made me feel
closer to my parents, I felt at home there.' Ambreen admits
that many may call her a traitor for feeling this way for a so-
called enemy state but she is not reserved in asserting her
affiliation with India. 'My roots are there. How can I not feel
at home?' she says. 'It feels so familiar, so comfortable. I had
heard so much from my parents that I felt like I had already
seen India before even going there. Although I never realized
it, these places have been a part of me since my childhood.'

I ask Ambreen if any of her other siblings want to visit
their parents' home as well. She had already convinced her

sister to come along but did they feel as strongly as she did? 'My little sister had a wonderful time going to Darya Ganj. We shared that emotional experience together in 2007, hugging and crying till we were exhausted. My brother also wants to go; he kept asking us about the areas when we returned. He said, *"bohat dil karta hai janey ka magar dar lagta hai keh shahid wapis aney ka dil hi na chahe"* (I really want to visit but I'm afraid that I may not ever want to return from there), so there is definitely this desire to go back in all of us. It is because of how our parents spoke about it.'

Both Ambreen's father and mother were saved from the worst of Partition. While they had to leave behind their homes and neighbours, they were saved from the butchering and murders. They were able to move together to Pakistan—without losing each other—and start a family. When Saghira Begum spoke about 1947, she would recall her childhood years, the people and dreams that had been left behind. Afzal Zaidi would reminisce about his Sikh friends. And so, while Ambreen grew up in the divided subcontinent, her parents' past meant that she and her siblings were not taught to express hatred towards India in their home or forced to see it as the enemy state. Today, this has shaped the relationship they hold with India; it has become the basis of their connection and continued association with the 'other'.

But, as Ambreen says, making the trips isn't easy. Hostile visa policies stand in the middle. 'I am lucky I'm married to Ramiz and that through him my sister and I were able to go. Otherwise, perhaps I would never have been able to. My parents' friends, even those whose passports say, "Born in Delhi," are unable to go to their homes without a credible invitation from India, so common people like me barely have a chance. Even for my brother it will be a huge hassle.' Shaking her head in disappointment, she says, 'So many people died during Partition but that is in the past now. A friend of my parents lost his wife and two children to the violence during migration and although he settled in Pakistan and remarried, that bitterness stayed with him. I can understand that but the bloodshed was on both sides and it's time we let go of those horrible memories. We can't allow this bitterness to travel to the new generations. It must be stopped.'

Her voice is racing against her; I can sense desperation in her. Ambreen, like thousands of other Pakistani and Indian men and women, has her past and present divided in between the two lands and the unfriendly government policies do not help.

'Till she died my mother thought one day the unpleasantness would subside . . . she would say, "this moment will pass and we'll go back home". I don't know how many more people from her generation must feel this way. How horrible it must be to not be able to go to your home. My mother carried that grief with her till the end. The only thing that would make her happy was to be able to talk about her *Dilli*. Then she would take out the saris and the *kundan* jewellery she had brought from there after Partition. She even had this *takozy* (tea pot cover) and a pillow she had embroidered herself as a child. The cover said "Good Morning" while the pillow had "Good Night" written across it . . .' Ambreen's voice trails off and I can tell that she is once again lost in her mother's world, far away from Pakistan and even further away from her present home in England. She is in Darya Ganj and no visa restriction can prevent her from being there.

chapter nine

THE TRAIN AT PUL BANGASH
RANA KAMAL UD-DIN AND
OWAIS RANA

'I am from Delhi but I have never been to Delhi.' This was Rana Kamal Ud-Din's answer to the chief executive of Jet Airways India, whom he met at a social gathering in Lahore. He had been so engrossed in describing Delhi and its people, that Naresh Goyal was convinced Rana hailed from India's capital. Little did he know that Rana had never been to Delhi. With his Pakistan Army background, he may never have a chance to go there either.

Visas for the other side are not easy for ordinary people to get, and army backgrounds render them even more difficult. Army officers are perceived as symbols of state nationalism and defence and hence, symbols of hatred and suspicion from the other side. Serving officers who want to travel across need to apply for special permission and No Objection Certificates, they have to answer a series of additional questions, they have to get background checks run on them and their family members. All of these reasons had prevented Rana from being able to visit during his service. Now that he is retired, he wants to actively pursue going across but on the day I speak with him, this remains only a wish.

He tells me that he grew up hearing stories about Delhi. He has relatives in the city. Pul Bangash, located in Kishanganj, Delhi, is his mother's first home. But till today the only Delhi he has seen is through modern technology—the media and Google Maps. He has spent hours trying to locate Kishanganj, to glance at Pul Bangash. For now, that is the only snapshot he is likely to get. The remaining are scraps of black and white photographs glued together in family albums, some lost, others damaged over the years.

Rana Kamal Ud-Din is the son of the late Razia Begum. Hailing from a Lucknow family, the Motiwalas—as they were called—shifted to Delhi in the early 1900s. It was here that Razia was born and lived until she was seventeen. But in 1947, she was uprooted like numerous other families and told to leave her home immediately—for to leave one's home was often the only window of survival during the hysteria of Partition.

Arriving in the unknown streets of Lahore, Razia was utterly lost. She was a pure Hindustani, says Rana, Urdu-speaking, and she could never quite learn Punjabi, the lingua franca of Lahore, or the Lahori Urdu, which is transfused with elements of Punjabi. 'Woh bari salees aur proper Urdu mein baat karti theen aur hamesha humein kehti theen kis zaban mein baat kar rahe ho? Urdu mein baat karo!' (She used to speak very sophisticated Urdu and always asked us what language we were speaking in, instructing us to talk in proper Urdu), laughs Rana.

Rana is one of the five children of Razia and Rana Muhammad Amin, a Lahori that Razia was married off to when she arrived in Pakistan. He tells me that his father's side of the family had lived in Lahore for at least two centuries. 231 Circular Road, located near Bhatti Gate of what is now Old Lahore, had been home to generations of the Rana family.

'Circular Road was the Ring Road of the old times,' says Rana. 'It was the first Ring Road of Lahore and it went all around the Walled City. I was also born in the same house, at 231 Circular Road, and lived there until the 1980s.' He repeats the address, the numbers and words crisp against his tongue. It was at the same Circular Road that Rana sat by his mother's feet in the evenings, listening to the few but clear memories she had of her childhood. As a woman from a conservative family, Razia Begum rarely stepped out of her house. She did not go to school either. As a young girl and later as a teenager, the house she lived in, the *mohalla* that surrounded her, the grounds that she played in came to constitute her small but happy world. The railway line in front of her house, the sounds of the trains trolling past Pul Bangash, the *nautankis* (theatre) that would liven up the neighbourhood, were the fragments of her past that Razia brought with her to Pakistan. It is these memories that have trickled down through her to her children. This is how most of them imagine Delhi: *wohi bade bade maidaan, wohi rail ki patri, wohi galiyaan* (the big grounds, the railway tracks, those alleys).

'Luckily they were saved from the misery others had to face while travelling to Pakistan on foot or by train,' Rana says softly, his eyes tender as he speaks about his mother. 'They were able to get a flight from Delhi to Lahore. I don't know how my *mamu* (uncle) arranged it but he did and that's how all of them escaped the worst of Partition.'

'My mother's elder sister, our *badi khala*, Sadeeqan, was

already married in Lahore to the Naqi Market people. They didn't have any children so the family stayed with her for some time. It was through her that they contacted my father's family and got my mother married off.

'There were so many changes in my mother's life and it took her a very long time to adjust. But even till the end some part of her was always stuck in Delhi, even if she never went back.' Rana is sombre as he says this but a few moments later breaks into laughter and surprises me as he makes a '*kooooo*' sound. I look up at him in amusement, the army man in front of me giggling in remembrance of his mother. He tells me that Razia would often make this sound to entertain the children. She would tell them that this was how the trains sounded as they passed by her house at night, waking the children and the elders from their deep slumber. 'She didn't know any English but she would always repeat this and *Hello Hello London Calling* from what she had heard on BBC radio as a child. She would say it in the perfect accent, and if we ever made fun of her she would tell us to shut up!' For a few seconds we both shake with laughter and I realize how much Rana must miss her, even seven years after her death. He was the closest to her out of his siblings.

'My mother was the youngest in her family,' he says after our laughter has subsided. 'Even her elder sister's kids were older than her. So she was really a child when she left India. But even still, she always recalled little things from her childhood—her friends, *mil keh baithna, kahaniyan sunna, bioscope camera se movie dekhna* (sitting together, listening to stories, watching movies from the bioscope camera). The cameraman would take money from four or five kids and show them a scene or a song from a movie. She would proudly say how late she would stay up on these nights to see the movies and theatre. It's remarkable that even when she got very unwell, towards the later stage of her life, she still remembered those days. She would sing the same songs she had learnt in Pul Bangash till the very end.'

As Rana says this I remember Iqbal sahib, who had accompanied Haroon and me to my interview at the border village with Naseer Ashiq (Chapter One). Iqbal sahib's wife had passed away just months ago in a roadside accident. In fact, she had died the very day that Iqbal sahib was meant to take Haroon and me back to Sheikpura to participate in the border mela that Naseer Ashiq had invited us to. Of course, the turn of events meant that the visit would have to wait until next year. What this also meant, however, was that Iqbal sahib's own mother seemed to lose her bearings. Shocked by her young daughter-in-law's death, she at first became angry and then deeply saddened by her loss. Disoriented, she began to insist that Iqbal sahib take her back to her village in Firozpur, India. When he tried explaining that she could not just get up and go but rather needed to obtain a passport and then a visa, she was utterly baffled. *'Passport ki kya zaroorat hai? Mera ghar hai woh. Chalo mujhe rasta aata hai, mein tum ko ja kar apna ghar dikhtati hoon.'* (Why do I need a passport to go to my home? Come, I know the way, I'll take you there and show you my home.) To the seventy-seven-year-old Fatima bibi, the idea of not being able to return, of borders and visas, made no sense. It is her home, she remembers the way, why can she not go back?

'This setback of moving from your house, of being uprooted like people were during Partition, can come back to haunt you at any time,' Iqbal sahib had said, and as I sit with Rana today, I realize that he was probably right. The memories, no matter how deep in the past they are, don't go away. The people, the rooms, the verandahs, remain etched in one's mind, whether as part of the subconscious or conscious. They will always be a part of the Partition survivors. As we lose more and more people from that generation, some of those memories are buried with them. But in conversations like these, those places and sounds, smells and people come alive once more. Today the *koooo* of Pul Bangash and the *Hello Hello* of BBC airing its way through Kishanganj no longer exist in India but they resonate as loudly in this small office in Lahore as they did all those years ago in Delhi.

'It is unfortunate that she could never go back. She used to keep unwell and didn't have the stamina for travel. Sometimes we would go to Karachi where all her brothers and sisters were living and even that was too much for her. But I always felt like I should go.' He explains that as his father lived in Lahore and Rana and his siblings were born in the same house as him, he never had any curiosity about his paternal roots. But as a child and then as an adult he always wanted to know more about his mother. He was inquisitive about where she had lived, where she had grown up. He tells me that even today, when he hears the name Delhi, he feels a sudden attachment, a connection. 'Whenever I meet anyone from Delhi, that's the first thing I tell them, that my mother was also from there. This cross-culture, inter-caste marriage between my mother and father, is the best thing that happened to our family. If we are interested in education or culture, it's because of India. We have always been inquisitive about the culture of Delhi, the culture of our mother . . . I mean, we lived in Bhatti where no one spoke Urdu . . .' he stops for a second to clarify that Lahori Urdu isn't the proper Urdu, in case I am confused. I nod quickly, as unsure as unwilling to question his confidence. That is the only Urdu I know but I am certainly not knowledgeable enough to argue about its authenticity or dialect. Assured that I understand what he means, Rana continues, 'People always get so shocked when we speak. They always ask us where we learnt to speak this way. I feel very fortunate about what my mother has taught us, the manners she has passed on.'

Language is just one of the many things that Rana has looked up to Razia for. He tells me that the way she sat, the way she ate, dressed and spoke all had an effect on them as young children. Delhi had crept into their upbringing. 'She had a musical sense in her culture, a household sense, an upbringing sense. All of that has affected us.'

But when Rana's cousin and Razia's nephew, Anwar, had a chance to go back and see his aunt's house after Partition, he was taken aback . . . The Pul Bangash he had so vividly imagined was nowhere to be seen. The closest he could get was Kishanganj and that too was far from what he had imagined. 'The manner in which my mother and uncle spoke about their neighbourhood had made us believe that it would be similar to Old Lahore but Anwar said it wasn't like that. It looked more like the recent constructions in Karachi; he didn't see any of the narrow lanes that we were expecting—it was nothing like the Delhi that we had thought about all these years. In fact, he said it was just like a place called Delhi Colony in Pakistan; it was nothing better than a slum.'

Delhi Colony—or the Delhi Sudagaran Colony—rests in the busy streets of Karachi, Sindh. People who had migrated from Delhi at the time of Partition had come to live here and went on to build a community to recreate, in whatever way they could, all that they had left behind. Legend has it that Punjabis who shifted to cities like Lucknow and Delhi for business purposes were referred to as the Punjabi Sudagaran. Becoming a sizeable community in Delhi, the Sudagarans were well-settled when Partition happened. Like the thousands of others around them, many of the Sudagarans too had to flee and came to inhabit Karachi, where their colony still thrives. Here they continue to be referred to as the *Dilliwalas*, their identity still cross-border. While in India I had heard about similar colonies. I was told that Lahore's elite and previously Hindu-dominated Model Town society had found its way to Delhi. There was a colony there by that name. For Anwar what this meant was that the Kishanganj that he saw was more like what he had seen all his childhood. It was not the Kishanganj of Razia and his father; rather, it was a replica of the migrant community resting in Pakistan itself.

Unable to locate the house or the street where his elders grew up, Anwar was about to return when he ran into a *lohar* (blacksmith) sitting by the roadside. Testing his luck, he decided to ask him whether he knew about Pul Bangash. The *lohar* looked up, his face creased with fine wrinkles, and asked, '*Kyun pooch rahe ho mian?*' (Why are you asking, sir?) When Anwar told him that his grandfather was from there the *lohar* put everything down and exclaimed, 'Where have you been?' Offering him tea he told him that he had known his family and had often wondered where they had gone, how they were. Unfortunately the house was no more, he said; the area had developed extensively, homes and memories lost in modern-day planning schemes.

Anwar is one of only two from the Motiwala family who has been able to return and see Kishanganj as it stands today.

The rest still have images created by the delicate words of
their parents and grandparents to cling on to. But Rana is the
other exception to this. He has done enough research, has
enquired from enough people to know that what he imagines
may not be there. His son Owais's recent visit to Delhi has
confirmed this. 'Owais brought back a video from that area
and I felt good . . . it felt good to see it even though it didn't
look anything like my mother had described. I missed her a lot
that day and thought if she were alive she would have been
delighted. She might not have been able to spot her house but
she would have seen Kishanganj, a familiar sign or building,
and felt that association . . . she would have been very happy to
see it again.'

I can see how much his mother's birthplace, his heritage
across the border, means to Rana. But at the same time, given
his army background and upbringing in Lahore, I cannot help
but wonder if this complicates his relationship with India.
After all, during Rana's service, India and Pakistan fought
several wars. Working in an army setting, where the mindset is
vehemently opposed to the 'other,' Rana has been forced to
fight his own mother's ancestral home time and time again. I
want to know how he makes sense of this home-yet-enemy
situation, how it feels to defend his present home against that
of the past. As I ask this, I believe that I have put forth an
extremely difficult question. I assume that it would take Rana
time to answer, to craft his words carefully, but it is me who is
caught off guard when he responds almost instantly.

'When you're in the army and you're fighting India, you're
not thinking of Delhi. You're only thinking of Lahore, of
Pakistan.' He says this point blank, looking straight into my
eyes, and I realize that Rana has already sorted out his emotions;

personal affiliations do not have space in professional capacity. That is the way he has been trained, as a second-generation Pakistani born and brought up in the divided subcontinent.

'The Pakistan Army is a defensive army; we have always been taught to protect Pakistan, to defend our country. Whenever we fought, whether 1971 or in Siachen, I didn't think I'd hit Delhi, I always thought that I'm here to defend Pakistan. I mean, I've met a lot of Indian officials who belonged to Lahore before Partition but they wouldn't think they're attacking their birthplace, they would think they're defending their country and that is rightly so.'

To me it seems like defending one's country against what was once home would be an unsettling task, to say the least. Contradictory, frustrating, alienating. But the way Rana tackles my question shows that for these officials, many of whom have a past across the border, the scenario is rather simple, in a way. Rana is not the only one to think this way. My own father served in the Pakistan Army for twenty years and despite his family's history and association with Batala, fought against the Indian side. Another family friend I had spoken to reiterated the same notion of defence. Being from the Partition generation itself, he was posted on the India-Pakistan border for several years after 1947. He told me that soldiers from both sides would often play sports, especially volleyball, and his Indian 'counterparts', as he called them, would even bring him his favourite brand of Indian cigarettes. Yet when the time came to fight, they fought tooth and nail. Such is the nature of the army; such are the dynamics between India and Pakistan, between home and enemy.

Owais, a friend and colleague—and son of Rana Kamal-Ud-Din—had travelled with me to India in October 2012. I had accompanied him while we searched through alleys and bylanes to find Pul Bangash for his father, asking passersby through our rolled-down windows for directions. Unfortunately, we were unable to locate Pul Bangash but after over an hour of searching and being stuck in peak-hour jampacked Delhi traffic, we were able to reach Kishanganj. Owais had taken out his camera and we had asked the driver to drive through the lanes slowly so that he could capture the streets for his father. I remember how each time we saw a sign or board reading Kishanganj, one of us would squeal and point towards it so that he could quickly shoot it, as legitimacy to his visit. We spent over thirty minutes driving through the same area before realizing that we were unlikely to get any further. We had no idea what to look for, what to ask; we were as lost as Anwar had been and unfortunately, despite us keeping our eyes open for the *lohar*, we didn't find him either. Perhaps he, too, like Razia Begum, was no more. Perhaps the last person to remember the Motiwalas had been lost as well.

For a while afterwards we had both been quiet; this was a rare site for the rather chirpy Owais and I wasn't sure how he felt. As a friend I knew that Owais did not have much interest in history but here he was, spending his Sunday in the buzzing city of Delhi to explore his roots. He had chosen to roam the alleys of Old Delhi on a burning afternoon over sleeping in an air-conditioned room or shopping for saris for his fiancé. Interest in history or not, his roots had sucked him in. As I sat behind him in the car, I wondered if I would ever be able to go back to Batala to see my father's ancestral home. I shook my head as I thought this, knowing that it was very unlikely. To come to Delhi, for business or leisure, made sense. I had friends here, I had my work here. In Batala I knew no one; I knew no addresses, no people. What reason did I have to go there? In all likelihood I never would. And so I sat behind and waited patiently for Owais to absorb what he had seen. This was perhaps the only participation I was going to have in tracing roots in India.

Back in Pakistan and speaking with Rana sahib, however, I realized that I should talk to Owais too. After all, he had experienced what his father had not. He had travelled where his father could not. I wondered how he understood his roots today, whether the meaning of Pul Bangash and Delhi had changed over the three generations in this family. After all, Owais, like me, has grown up in a Pakistan that is quite different from his father's.

For our generation, raised in the 1990s and 2000s, the political reality of India and Pakistan was far different from what our elders such as Malik Siddiqui (Chapter Five), Roshan Ara (Chapter Six) or Rana had experienced. The wars of 1965 and 1971 and then the heightened Kashmir conflict during the 1990s began to drastically change the fabric of society. The idea of India being accessible, of it requiring just a permit to cross over, began to give way to that of a country we had fought wars with, a country which refused to give us what the Pakistani state believed was rightfully theirs; a country which had not only taken away much of Kashmir but also helped East Pakistan break away.

TV transmission, which began in the mid-1960s, began to further highlight these issues, bringing them to the drawing rooms of ordinary people. Indo-Pak relations began to turn sour and by the 1990s, the time when Owais and I were in school, tensions were high. Anyone who grew up in the 1990s can recall the Kashmir Bulletin, which would play after prime-time news on the state-owned and most popular TV channel, PTV. News about atrocities committed by Indian soldiers was rampant across the country, with children as young as seven or eight absorbing the bloody telecast night after night.

Another transformative change that began in the 1970s was the revision of the educational curriculum. Whereas previously history covered both Hindu and Buddhist periods before introducing the arrival of Islam to the region, this period saw an overall Islamization of the curriculum, especially with the arrival of Pakistan Studies as a compulsory subject across schools. Soon, any history preceding Muhammad Bin Qasim was censored, and history thus began to be understood in terms of Islam purifying the region of infidel practices of the Hindus. President Zia-ul-Haq's National Educational Policy of 1979 further stated that 'the hightest priority would be given to the revision of the curricula with a view to reorganizing the entire content around Islamic thought and giving education an ideological orientation so that Islamic ideology permeates the thinking of the younger generation and helps them with the necessary conviction and ability to refashion society according to Islamic tenets.'[7]

Born in the late 1980s, Owais and I both became prime consumers of this curriculum as well as the mainstream discourse on television and newspapers. The narrative around India was changing. Increasingly, Pakistan was disowning its shared history and thereby endorsing and reinforcing the Two-

---

[7]National Commission for Justice and Peace (NCJP). *Education VS Fanatic Literacy* (Sanjh Publications, March 2013), p.5.

Nation theory, which had proved to be a catalyst for its creation in the first place. For young minds like ours, India was not a place where our ancestors had shared many happy moments, where they still had their homes, and at times family members, but rather a country synonymous with 'infidel' Hindus who we were better off without.

For me, my university experience in England and Canada, among Indian students, and interviewing people and collecting stories for my work at CAP began to unfold a slow process of unlearning and later, re-learning. I started to understand how much we had at stake across the border, not in terms of economics but because of personal histories, relationships and homes. I began to absorb how much cities like Delhi and Amritsar really meant to some of us Pakistanis. And I began to realize how much preceded the violence of Partition and how many bonds continue to be sustained despite the bloody event of 1947. Without this, I was indifferent even to Batala, my heritage. So indifferent that when Muhammad Rauf (Chapter Two) had told me he had visited Batala on the way to Qadian to attend the Ahmadiyya procession, I had not even bothered to ask what it was like, it had evoked nothing in me. I was more interested in his story, about his experience at the Wagah border, about the incomplete bus tour of Amritsar, his home.

I wondered what Owais's journey had been like. Being a generation apart from Rana and two from Razia Begum, what meaning did going back to his *dadi's* home have for him? I turned to him to ask some of these questions.

'While I was growing up I didn't hate Indians like a lot of my friends because my father always spoke positively about them. But studying in an army school, I definitely didn't consider them friends either.' I was not surprised to hear this.

It would be difficult for Rana to call his mother's home 'evil', as many other parents are easily able to do. Belonging to a family that was saved from the violence of Partition, Razia Begum's recollections of 1947 were mixed with nostalgia rather than animosity. She had spoken fondly of her childhood; Rana had been amused and in fact in awe of her culture. But while this prevented outright hatred in Owais and his siblings, he tells me that the material and conversations they were subjected to outside their homes continued to create a rift in their hearts against the neighbour. 'In school we would read about the massacres of Muslims in 1947 and how India tried to separate East Pakistan from us. And then my father would be posted away from home to fight wars with India so there was always this feeling of mistrust and resentment towards them.'

'Since he was posted away a lot, we didn't meet *dadi* very much either and I never really got to hear about her childhood in Delhi until much later. Until college I never even knew that she had migrated from India. It never came up.'

As a teenager, Owais was more intrigued by girls, video games and sports than stories of his grandmother, which seemed archaic to him. He was the ordinary grandchild; respectful of his grandparents but failing to believe that they could share anything more. Rana too, despite being so involved in his past, had not spoken to Owais about his unwavering association with Delhi. Perhaps he had not found it important; he thought it would be irrelevant to Owais. Perhaps Owais had never listened; he never gave his father the chance to share his mother's fondest memories. I wonder how many more families cut off that connection between their past and present by failing to speak of that which they hold so close to their hearts; is it purposeful or was it an oversight? Whichever it was, it meant that for Owais, Delhi was just the capital of

India; it was the archrival of Islamabad; it was the regional superpower, one that was making drastic economic advancements. That was the only link he could register with this 'other' for the majority of his waking years.

However, this began to change when Owais was given the chance to represent Pakistan in a conference in Bangalore. Rana's son had been invited to India; someone else from the Motiwala family was about to cross the line. 'My father was so happy that he distributed *mithai* in his office. I thought he was excited that I was travelling out of Pakistan for the first time but it wasn't that. It was the fact that I was going to India, to his mother's home. For the first time, I realized I shared a connection across the border but I don't think I understood what that meant. I remember thinking, alright, so *dadi* was born there, that's strange. But that was all, it was just a stab of realization that came and went.'

'In fact, I was far too nervous about leaving the country for the first time, and especially about travelling to India, of all the places. To me it was always like you can go anywhere in the world but you have to have a strong enough reason to go to India. I didn't think of it as a place for vacationing or fun and I kept questioning whether I had made the right decision by signing up for the conference. Plus the Mumbai attacks had just happened and Pakistan was being blamed so I was feeling more scared than anything else. I kept thinking about what their reaction would be when they saw my green passport. I guess I had generalized that everyone in India was the same: anti-Pakistan or at least unwelcoming.'

Clearing customs and breathing a sigh of relief, when Owais stepped out of the airport he was overwhelmed by the size of Bangalore. It was nothing like what he had expected. 'The conference was being held at The National Law University and we kept driving and driving for the longest time. I was used to airports being really close to one's home and for a while I actually thought I was being kidnapped!' he laughed as he said this but I know that a piercing fear must have gripped him at that moment. The popular image of travelling to India is that of forced imprisonment, abduction and disappearance cases. My own mother had been panic-stricken when I went to India for the first time even though I had spent over three years away from her at university, oceans away in Canada. 'India is different,' she said, 'one has heard so many frightening stories that it scares one.'

Fortunately for Owais, however, he was not kidnapped. Rather he was safely transported to the VIP hostel rooms booked for the delegation and was attended to immediately. 'It was a big beautiful campus but like any other public university in Pakistan. Even the students were just like the student body at my university back home.' It was almost I am by the time Owais reached the university but the Indian students stuck to him. 'I remember I wanted to smoke but it wasn't allowed on campus so they actually escorted me out in the middle of the night. It kind of broke the ice. I realized that we weren't really poles apart as I had thought.'

The week-long conference gave Indians and Pakistanis a chance to quell their curiosity. They could ask questions that had been buzzing in their minds; they could engage in debates over drinks and *vada pao* late into the night; they could finally know the 'other' through the 'other'. It was during this trip that Owais began to learn more about the neighbour he shared geography and history with; a neighbour which was always the focal point in his home and country but one that he had never wished to delve into.

But when I ask if in the midst of all this he felt a sense of belonging, a familial connection with India, he shakes his head. 'Not really. I spent a night in Delhi but I didn't feel anything. Before I left for India my dad had said, "you're one-fourth from Delhi so get to know the city," but I had no time and I guess I wasn't keen either. It was only when I returned and saw how disappointed my father was that I promised myself I would make it a point to visit the next time I was in Delhi.'

This promise came true the fall of the same year. 'This time when we went to India for the CAP project, I decided I was going to make a video for my father. I'm glad I could document the place before it changes even more. By doing so, I feel I have provided a service to my family. I have brought back a little bit of my *dadi* for them. But if you ask me if going back changed anything for me, I don't think it did. Kishanganj means as much to me or as little, perhaps, as Bhatti Gate, where my father grew up. I remember as a child my father once took me there, to his house at 231 Circular Road, where he had lived until 1980. I was ten years old and the house had turned yellow, it had become a printing press. I didn't get why my father was so happy to see this old building, what the big deal was. Unfortunately, as a family we never discussed roots and by the time I found out about my *dadi's* past it was already too late . . . she was no longer alive to tell me more.'

Blushing, Owais confesses that when he had replayed the shots from Kishanganj he realized that the reflection of the windscreen had been a constant disturbance in the video, an obstruction to seeing whatever little he had taped. He felt bad, he says, but it is also unlikely that he will ever go back there. He has fulfilled his obligation, his duties as Razia Begum's grandson by recreating the past, albeit with some blurriness. As he said, he had served his family.

chapter ten

A PUNJABI WITHOUT ROOTS

ALPANA KISHORE

It is the fall of 2012. It has been two days since I arrived in India. I decide to leave my colleagues to shop at the luxurious Select City Mall in Saket, close to where we are staying, and step into a white taxi outside, to make my way to Alpana Kishore's house near Lodhi Road. I met Alpana, an Indian journalist, at a conference I attended in Delhi to discuss peace initiatives between India and Pakistan . Although much of her experience was in Jammu and Kashmir, Alpana mentioned the work she had started years ago, on Partition and migration on both sides of the border. It was a project she was unable to complete because of lack of funding and hostile Indo-Pak relations through the 1990s, but one that she said she still considered very close to her heart.

With a glass of mint lemonade and a plate of Oreos placed in front of me, I sink comfortably into a large suede couch across from Alpana as she sips her hot cup of tea. It's about 5 pm and I start off by asking her more about her work, about what moved her to explore Partition. I am excited to speak with an Indian journalist—the voices of Indian journalists are often lost in the Pakistani narrative, and vice versa. This one-on-one is a novelty for me.

'Well, I have Punjabi roots. My grandmother, Vimla Virmani, studied in Kinnaird College, Lahore, and my *nana*, Hansraj Virmani, had mills in Okara that continued running until about 1965,' she begins. 'My grandmother's father was Gokul Chand Narang, a minister in the Unionist government and so the maternal side of my family was very prominent. They ran breweries, banks and sugar mills, leaving behind everything at the time of Partition. My mother too had been born in Faisalabad, then Lyallpur, so for me there was always much to explore about Partition, a rupture that had taken away much of my own heritage.'

Soon after she became a journalist, Alpana decided to research more on 1947, specifically why some people had decided to migrate while others stayed back, in India or Pakistan. She wanted to study the 'choice' narrative, the stories of those migrants who had not been forced to flee but rather had chosen to do so by their own free will. Her first trip to Pakistan took her to Lahore, her ancestral city. It was 1992, just before the Babri Mosque incident, and Alpana was part of a delegation of journalists that was meant to cover different aspects of Pakistani politics. I ask her if there was a particular purpose to their visit and she responds with a smile, 'It was Pakistan. You didn't need anything special, everything made news.'

Alpana, who desperately wanted to see both the Narang House in Lahore—where her grandparents had spent much of their lives—as well as the Sundaywali Kothi in Faisalabad— where her mother was born—was delighted to be able to visit at least one of them. And so, at the first chance she got, she made her way to the Narang House.

'It was situated on Montgomery Road and had been converted into a nurses' hostel. Anam, you would be surprised but the Narang study was just the same as before, just the way my grandparents had described it. It even had the same books, the same carpet and my grandfather's desk! And outside there was a lovely courtyard, with a big Hindu-style fountain in the middle. I cried when I saw it. It was a huge, huge sense of loss.'

She pierces her lower lip with her teeth, but after a moment her melancholic voice gives in to a giggle and she says, 'Let me tell you a hilarious story. My two cousins from Doon School once visited Lahore for a squash tournament at Aitchison College and also decided to visit the house. They had just begun to look around and snap a few photographs when the guard pounded on them. He was convinced that they were young boys, ogling at the nurses!' Her laugh is hearty but touched with nostalgia. Many of the migrant families I have spoken to in Pakistan, no matter what city or class they belong to, expressed a sorrow, a sadness when they spoke about their lost homes, their roots. I can see the same sentiments resonate in Alpana.

I ask her if she tried going to Faisalabad too, to see her mother's home. 'No, I couldn't. I didn't have the visa. I've still not seen it but I haven't stopped trying either,' she smiles. When I offer to visit it for her and take some pictures, she is elated and rushes to give me the details. 'That would be absolutely wonderful! I don't know what the address is but I do know my grandfather used to run a school over there, which he later reopened in Roop Nagar, Delhi. It was called the Dhanpat Mal Virmani School and I hear it's been converted into the Islamia School but still has the same Hindu structure, with the big Arya Samaj symbol on the top. Maybe you could ask for that!'

I nod and ask her if her grandparents ever spoke about what the Faisalabad *kothi* looked like. I expect elaborate details about the rooms, the gardens, the lifestyle. These would perhaps help me relocate the house for her. Instead, Alpana astonishes me with a one-word answer, 'Never,' she says. I stop writing and look up, 'Never?' She leans forward in her seat and repeats, 'No, never. I would have to probe again and again to find out whatever little I do know about Partition, about the Sundaywali Kothi, about the Narang house. Even when I returned after seeing it and told my *nani*, she just said, "Was it nice?" As if I had gone for a vacation to a completely unfamiliar place.'

'Partition was a huge trauma. If I had to leave Delhi today and never come back I would be devastated. That is what happened with them but for some reason they never spoke about it, not unless I really forced them to. I would ask my *nani* about her Muslim friends and she would tell me *"koi nahi tha"* (there were none). It was only when I kept pestering her that details about some Fatimah or Syeda would come up. Even my own brother couldn't care less about it. Nor have I ever heard my mother speak about it. It is as if it doesn't exist for her either. We are an elite family by many standards but we have all forgotten where we come from. No one even refers to it.'

In 1986 Alpana's *nani* went back to Lahore for an event at Kinnaird College. 'I had thought she would come back overwhelmed but she was unaffected. She spoke about her visit so coldly, as if she had been to some completely foreign land, Poland or France! I think as a community they just cut it off, there was a hardening, a finish.' She stops for a moment and then says, 'It is unfair to us, to the succeeding generations. There is no inkling about our land, our soil, culture. We have lost it completely.' She tells me that for years one could not speak about Partition or Pakistan in the public space. There was no movie on it either. *Garam Hawa* was one of the first ones and that too was about the Muslim narrative. 'Our trauma was never heard or discussed. It was almost as if we never felt it.'

I am trying to wrap my head around everything she is saying. It was true that even in many of the families I had spoken with in and around Lahore, several did not want to talk about Partition. They wanted to put it behind them; it was too painful to go down that memory lane. However, it was also a reality that they couldn't forget or disengage from. In my own home, while my grandmother may not have spoken about her Hindu friends Rajeshvari and Uma, just as Alpana's grandmother did not speak about Fatimah or Syeda until probed, for decades I was subjected to stories of violence, loss and brutality. Partition always had a way of lingering over our family discussuons. For others like Rana (Chapter Nine), Ambreen (Chapter Eight) and Intikhab (Chapter Seven), the losses and homes they left behind made it to dinner-table coversations.

And even if families remained silent about the topic, Partition came to be discussed through other channels—in literature, media, curriculum, public discourse, woven in the very fabric of the society. The Two-Nation theory, which became the basis of the split of the Indian subcontinent, is endorsed tacitly or overtly by all political parties in Pakistan, it is taught in schools, it is dominant in the mainstream narrative. Perhaps because Partition was an event that led to the creation of Pakistan, it was something that could not be avoided, denied or ignored. However, Alpana's experience seems to have been different, which makes me wonder all the more why she cares so much about Partition. As someone belonging to the third generation in India post-Partition, what made her so involved that even her work came to reflect it?

'As a child I studied with many Punjabis and non-Punjabis at my school,' she says. 'In the holidays they would all return to their native villages and cities but I had no place to go. I had no link to my ancestral home, to any part of that land. I had lost that connection completely, even the language. My *nani* used to speak to her sisters and husband in Punjabi but she refused to talk with my mother in any other language but Hindi. I think she was afraid. She would tell her that if she didn't know the national language, it would be divisive . . . so I guess if you are in a void, you are more curious. I knew nothing. *Koi baat hi nahi karta tha.* This veil of silence, or indifference— whatever you want to call it—made no sense to me. So I started to dig deeper.'

I stop to think whether Muhammad Ali Jinnah thought along the same lines when he refused to incorporate Bengali as a state language but Alpana interrupts me. 'You know, Anam, you feel that loss every day. Even today, I yearn to speak Punjabi but Indian Punjabi is *jatt* rural Punjabi. West Punjabis spoke it in a sophisticated way, like the Lahoris. That's the physical loss of Partition,' she sighs. 'Sometimes I try and sit next to people who speak that Punjabi because I don't hear it anymore. That's the quantified loss. No one uses the word *okha* anymore. I remember my grandma used to say it to my *nana* whenever they had a fight, *Tussi okhay kyun ho rahe ho?* (Why are you getting haughty with me?) Sometimes I use it but only my husband gets it. These words step away from you. They are gone. It upsets me terribly that my children will never know them. The language, our heritage has been ripped away from all of us.'

'Do you think your grandparents don't want to talk about it because it is too tragic? It's too painful to revisit their past? I've experienced that with many Partition suvivors in Pakistan,' I tell her.

'No, you can't say it was because of the trauma of Partition. My *nana-nani* lived fantastic lives in Delhi, in complete Punjabi style. My *nani* would wear her exquisite chiffon saris, they would go play bridge, go to parties. Of course they struggled initially. They had lost everything in Pakistan, their mills, distribution points, everything. They had to start from scratch. But they came and built a whole new life and looking at them, you'd never know they were traumatized. So I really don't know what that indifference was. And it was present in everyone's grandparents, not just mine.

'I've thought about it a lot and I think that when a whole society suffers, you have your friends, family and extended community to suffer with you, to feel your grief. It's something that only happens once in a generation or hundreds of years. It's an epochal migration. A storm that uproots you but everyone around you is also in the same boat. So questions about how to survive, where to live—they all figure it out together. Maybe that's why they managed to remain so indifferent.' Perhaps it was just that. It was the way the whole community healed. But why didn't we see similar notions on the other end, in Pakistan? Alpana answers this for me before I even put forth the question.

'You know we Punjabis are very different people, even different from other Indians. There is a cultural sense of not belonging here. You feel at home in Delhi only because there are so many Punjabis here but elsewhere, in UP and other states, you feel out of place. Most Indians are not as flamboyant, they don't have large gestures or the Punjabi loudness in them. They are subdued, they don't even share our sense of humour. We believe in taking life by its horns and just enjoying it. We are an irreverent race and perhaps that is another reason why Partition has also become something we don't take seriously, we push it aside. Our grandparents freed us of that burden, of remembering Punjab as it existed sixty-five years ago.' Pouring herself some more tea, she carries on the conversation, 'Punjab has been raided so many times during the seventeenth and eighteenth centuries that maybe it has taught us to ignore invasions. Kashmiris, on the other hand, hold on, sticking to their misery. We were never told to stick to anything or I'd still be thinking of going back to Lyallpur!' She chuckles, 'But instead, we never looked back. That is a tragedy but in a way I'm also free from that baggage. This is a Punjabi thing, though. It doesn't exist for other communities, nor for the mohajirs (migrants) in Karachi because they were never fully accepted.'

I ask Alpana to elaborate on what she means by her comments on the mohajirs. I have only spoken to the migrants settled in and around Lahore and want to know more about her experience of working among the largely Urdu-speaking migrant community in Karachi.

'Well I spent a lot of time with the mohajirs of Karachi when I was doing my work on Partition. They were the people who had *chosen* to move, not because they suffered violence but because that is what they wanted to do. But when they began to suffer in Pakistan, it became their basis of looking back. It was very difficult for them to adjust after expecting something completely different. Of course, they knew that they were better off than they would have ever been in India. They had arrived in a newly-made country that needed to fill a massive number of government posts. And since there were not many qualified people in the country, several migrants got jobs at posts higher than what they had in India. They would even brag to their families back in India, those who had chosen to stay behind. And movies like *Garam Hawa* reiterated that notion of the "Ideal Pakistan", portraying life as so much better for the Muslims on that side of the border. And it's true, life was indeed better for them, in the fifties and even the sixties. While their relatives in India were still stuck in the same place with the same plodding pace of life, often at low posts, the mohajirs had catapulted ahead. But then as the second generation started to grow up, many of them began to regret their parents' choice of migration. They had started to face the anti-mohajir spirit once the real sons of the soil, the Punjabis, started dominating, garnering power and government jobs due to their sheer numbers and the fact that they were rooted in the soil. The mohajirs had thought they would be the chosen ones but after the initial advantage that they had, they began to get identified with their *old* country, India. The second generation started to ask, What would have happened, had we stayed on the other side? Meanwhile, the first generation had another kind of regret, that Pakistan had never turned out to be as they had imagined.

'This was similar to how a lot of the first-generation Indian Muslims regretted their choice of staying back. They idealized Pakistan, wished they could be there. They would clap for Pakistan and support them in all matches and tournaments.

What that eventually resulted in was Hindu resentment, an urge to rid India of such Muslims whom they saw as traitors. And on the other hand, back in Karachi, this led to another kind of suffering—that is, regret—which has kept them from moving on, from ridding themselves of the baggage of Partition. That's the difference between us Punjabis and them. We have let go while they continue to cling on to what happened, what they chose, sixty-five years ago.'

Alpana's work and experience is insightful. Whether one should have stayed back or taken the plunge are questions that must be in the hearts of many on both sides of the border. Perhaps this void, this indifference to the past, is also true for many Indians and Pakistanis. However, at the same time, there are other voices to be heard, other stories to be told. From taxi drivers to teachers to politicians, I had interacted with many Indians who had Pakistani roots and were desperate to hear more about it, to be able to picture the land of their parents and grandparents. They would ask me to speak with them in Punjabi, they would ask me if I knew this road or that area in Pakistan; their parents were from 'that' side, they said. Many of them were Indian Punjabi migrants like Alpana's grandparents, but unlike them, Pakistani cities were still alive and burning in their hearts. Visiting it, being a part of it, 'completed' them. I had also interviewed many Punjabi migrants in Pakistan who had expressed the trauma of Partition, who had wanted to talk about the losses of that time. And while I had not worked directly with the Urdu-speaking migrants of Karachi, I can take the liberty to assume that several of them would not regret their choice of moving, despite the conflict, nor would all first-generation Indian Muslims want to move to Pakistan. But these generalizations

I would be wary of making given the limited time I have spent in India, and especially since I was unable to speak to Alpana's grandparents directly. Their story might have been different; the way it might have travelled over the generations at variance with what they had felt and experienced. Perhaps they didn't seem traumatized to Alpana only because they repressed that trauma effectively in front of their children and grandchildren. Perhaps it was too painful to share the past, as it is for many Partition survivors in Pakistan. I would never know and perhaps, neither would Alpana.

I ask Alpana to tell me more about her experience of travelling to Pakistan. To me, the experience people had of crossing over, not as a community but as individuals, was insightful and Alpana's experience was as important as any other. 'I went in wearing rose-tinted glasses but they came off fast. People were very hostile to me, especially in Lahore. They were hospitable alright, polite too, but over and over again I would be made to feel "Hindu". I was made to feel conscious of my religious identity.' She seems a little flushed, as if still angry at the thought of having made to feel this way. 'I had never felt like that in secular India. Yes, after the Hindutva movement there was a sense of "*those* are Muslims" but I had grown up in a lovely India, where there were no such distinctions. There were few Muslims in Delhi then, at least from my class, and I had never questioned anyone's patriotism because of their religion. But here I was described as "*you Hindu*", and it was a very strange feeling. I had never been described like that before.'

I am not surprised to hear this. While I have always been

welcomed warmly in India, my friends have narrated incidents
of discrimination on both sides of the border. One of my
colleagues had been told at four different hotels in Delhi that
they were unwilling to house a Pakistani. A taxi driver told
one of my friends to get off mid-way after hearing he was from
Lahore. Such episodes have the capability of further
entrenching stereotypes and hatred for the 'other'. Alpana
realizes this, 'I'm sure this kind of hostility has happened to
Pakistanis travelling to India as well. The Kashmir issue was
burning during the early nineties when I was visiting and
there was minimal exchange between the two countries so I
can't blame them but it was still a very uncomfortable
experience. I ended up coming back with a very different sort
of relationship with Pakistan. My boss, who had Punjabi roots,
had told me I'd hate it, that I'd be disappointed. That was sort
of true.

'Partition started to make sense to me, unlike before. I still
wish it had never happened, but if it had to, I'm glad it
happened back then; that it's behind us and we don't have to
deal with it now. Otherwise we would still be grappling with
all those issues.' Had Partition not taken place, she feels that
the growing extremism in Pakistan today would have been
blamed on Muslims not having their own country, on 'Hindu
discrimination' or 'second-class citizenship'. 'Those arguments
would have crippled this country before it could even start
taking its baby steps. Our notion of development and our idea
of what the country should be was very different from what
the founding fathers of Pakistan wanted and it would have
torn us into little pieces constantly fighting over the vision of a
united India. I just feel that it's good that it happened at the
start of independence itself and we were all able to move on, in
our own ways.'

In all likelihood, many people in India and Pakistan endorse this line of thinking, whether because they actually believe in the reasons for which Pakistan was created or because of how their opinions have been shaped as a result of subsequent oral history transmissions, state nationalistic agenda or the jingoistic patriotism promoted by the media. In either case, there is minimal public space to engage in such discourse, to question the reasoning of the forefathers. What is then perhaps more interesting is how, despite popular opinion, the nostalgia, the wistfulness and longing for one's roots on the other side are still alive, still burning in so many hearts on both sides of the border. 'The hostility is political,' Alpana says, 'but the emotional cord cuts through that hostility.' It was this emotional link that took her back to Pakistan twice more, in 2003 and 2005.

It was during these two visits that Alpana began to interact with more and more locals, in Lahore and Karachi. 'I began to feel at home, especially the last time I went in 2005. The shopkeepers, the people on the streets, everyone was lovely and we'd have such wonderful conversations. It was then that I began to see the immense similarity in our lifestyles. The way we have our breakfasts, the way we speak, it's so similar that it shocks you.' She lets out a hearty laugh and says, 'My husband has this habit of calling all servants *beta* (child), he even ends up calling people older than him *beta*! It was only in Pakistan that I saw that too. There was this uncanny resemblance which just astonishes you.'

'You know, West Punjab is part of our civilization, our heritage and I can never claim it. That part of my heritage, which defines me, can never be mine again. I can never assert rights on it. It's the same for the mohajirs in Pakistan. When you cut off a plant from its roots, the flowers begin to grow in different ways. That's how we are today, each walking aimlessly to find some sense of belonging. I still have this overwhelming association for Lahore, for Lyallpur, and I'm the third generation. But no matter what I do, or don't do, that part of me is lost forever. My children won't know that they came from Lyallpur—and even if I tell them, it wouldn't matter to them.' Taking in a deep breath, she hugs me tightly and we begin to say our goodbyes. I wish there was something I could say to reassure her, to tell her that her heritage isn't lost. But I also know that Alpana's fears are valid. With the handful of people who cross over and with India and Pakistan both losing the Partition generation so rapidly, many of those links would go untapped; they would be lost forever. I was only three when both my paternal grandparents passed away; I never heard what Batala meant to them, and my father was too young at Partition to share his family's past with me. Just as I would never know the importance of my ancestral city, Alpana's teenagers may never know the moments and the events that made the Narang House and Sundaywali Kothi pulsate with life for years. Lahore and Lyallpur only exist through their mother today, and when slowly they fade away with her, her children are unlikely to feel even a pinch of grief.

chapter eleven

HITLER'S DOG

RAFAY ALAM

'"*Haramzade, tu merey ghar mein rehta hai!*" (You rascal, you live in my home!) Martand literally barged into my room one day and started yelling. I thought he had truly lost it!' Rafay crouches forward in his chair, his hand gesturing wildly as he narrates this fiction-like story to me. Martand, who is from India, was not only one of Rafay's closest friends in England, where he was studying at Lincoln's Inn, but also a housemate at William Goodenough House, an international housing facility boasting students from all over the world. What Rafay and Martand did not know for the longest time, however, was that they shared an affiliation that crossed oceans and boundaries, a relationship rooted not only in Rafay's city, Lahore, but also his home, 90 Upper Mall.

I have known Rafay since 2010. The Citizens Archive of Pakistan (CAP) is one of the organizational boards he is a member of and during my time at CAP, I found him to be one of the easiest board members to get along with. We had many lunches and chatted over several cups of coffee, discussing work but more so, fresh ideas and thoughts. Whenever the topic turned towards history, one could be certain that the story of 90 Upper Mall, the house where he had grown up and continued to stay in, would come up. Rafay, thrilled to have any opportunity to share the rather fascinating story about his house, was unstoppable once he started.

I knew that he lived in what was referred to as evacuee property and that a famous Hindu irrigation engineer, Bawa Natha Singh, had something to do with it. Yet someone would always interrupt and the conversation would jump from one subject to another. Each time I would return home with a vague idea about the house, intrigued but never fully informed. Wanting no intrusions this time around, I asked Rafay if I could come see him after work at his house over one more cup of coffee. Rafay is a busy man and I'm happy to have an evening with him all to myself. I can finally know the almost legendary tale of this house.

'That's how you found out that this was Martand's family's house before they moved to India at Partition? What was your reaction? Were you shocked? Happy? Confused?' I bite my tongue as I say this, realizing that the interviewing skills I have developed over the past few years seem to have gone on a long holiday today. I think this is probably the first time that somebody else is more excited to hear this story than Rafay is to tell it. To live in evacuee property is routine business for Pakistanis given the influx of migrants that overflowed the country after Partition. But to be able to identify the previous residents, and that too in one's closest friend, is simply remarkable.

My own father had told me that when his family migrated from Batala to Lahore, they too had moved into evacuee property, at 45 McLeod Road. As a child, it was a strange concept for me to understand; to move into someone's home without their permission. I used to wonder what would happen if the previous owners ever came back to see or claim their home but my father would laugh and gently explain, 'It's not so easy, *beta,* just like I can't go back to Batala, they can't come here. Don't worry, I'm sure they bought another home.' Later, as an adult, when I would hear my father talk about how he missed his McLeod Road home, how he wished his family had never sold it to hotel owners, I wondered how much the Hindu family must miss it too. As naïve as it was, for years I worried how they would feel if they came back and saw it had been converted into a hotel, whether they would even be able to recognize it. But over time I realized such things did not happen. Those who left might never find out what happened to their homes; they were barely ever able to return. The reality faced by Muhammad Rauf (Chapter Two) and others like him was far more common; death often came quicker than another glimpse of their home.

But Rafay and Martand's story seems to be different. Martand has discovered who lives in his family's house; Rafay has found the history of 90 Upper Mall. They have uncovered links that most people never come across. I lean forward to hear more about their experience, my pen perfectly poised to scribble down his answer.

'I remember I turned around and said, "How the hell do you know?" But I think more than anything else, I was just astounded.' He pauses to reach besides him and picks up a notebook, 'I took out my journal from my years in college to share with you and I was just reading about that day. Surprisingly, I didn't write much. It just says: 22 *April 2000: I live in Martand's grandfather's house, Martand's father tells me.* And then I carry on talking about some other stuff. I think it was too strange a concept to digest.'

I'm a little disappointed that there were no dramatic tears and hugs but decide to return to 22 April after a while. There is much more to know before that. 'Rafay, first tell me about this house. Tell me about its history, how it even links to Martand's family?'

'Well Martand always likes to start the story with Hitler's dog,' he laughs. 'Hitler's dog? Let me get this straight, there is Pakistan, India, Britain *and* now Germany involved *too* in this story?'

'Well yes, Hitler's dog has quite the central role to play,' he grins and takes a sip of his whisky as I reach for my coffee. I really don't know what to expect from this interview anymore. I decide to put my pen and paper on the side and lean back with my cup, ready to be amused further. 'You see, Hitler had a litter of puppies in the late 1930s which he gave to various friends, allies, world leaders,' Rafay says casually, as if it's the most ordinary story. He has probably told it so many times that it's become a routine part of his narration. 'One of these managed to come down to the kingdom of Afghanistan and was given to a *hakeem*—a Muslim doctor of the king. At that time if you were a doctor, you knew every other doctor in the area. My great-grandfather, who was also a doctor in the British army, knew this gentleman. He eventually received the dog from him but as it wasn't much to his liking, he passed it on to my grandfather. That was how it came to be known as Hitler's dog.'

The story is fascinating indeed. From Germany to Afghanistan to India, the dog must have had quite an eventful journey. Yet I'm still uncertain how this connects to Rafay's house or to Martand's sudden outburst on that late April afternoon.

'Well, Hitler's dog grew up in Delhi and people from all over would come to see him. Qurban Ali Khan, the SP of the city, was one of them. Later, when he was posted as IG Punjab following Partition, it was through the dog's story that he traced my grandparents. Alarmed that they were still living with Colonel sahib—my grandmother's father—he quickly processed an evacuee property application for them and got them this house. But look at this place!' Rafay exclaims, 'It's ridiculously huge. He must have used all his influence to get a place of this size!'

He is probably right. Located opposite Lahore Gymkhanna, the house has two entrances that go around a whole block. The garden, where Rafay's grandmother, Surraiya Alam, runs Pakistan's first Montessori, stretches from one corner to the other. Rafay, his parents and his grandparents live in separate portions of the house; ample space divides them in between and yet the rooms are spacious, so is the patio where we are sitting this evening.

'How much did you know about the history of this house before you met Martand?'

'Well, I knew it was evacuee property, allotted to my grandfather after Partition. I figured it must have belonged to Hindus or Sikhs before Partition and then I had vague recollections that Salima Hashmi, my aunt, had apparently met the owners of this house upon one of her visits to India. But that was pretty much it. Whenever we spoke about the house we would talk about Hitler's dog because that was always more entertaining.'

At the time of Partition, Rafay's grandfather was working for Bird & Co., a leading trading house in India. A witness to the splurges of violence and bloodshed in Delhi, the company decided to send the Muslim couple off to Lahore, far away from the anti-Muslim mobs. However, soon Mr and Mrs Alam, as they were called, moved back to Bombay, where Rafay's grandfather started his training for his new job at the Associated Cement Company. It was only in 1953 that the couple shifted permanently to Pakistan, and specifically Lahore, where Mrs Alam's parents had already come to settle soon after 1947. A fantastic tennis player, and in fact the only person to have played Wimbledon both as an Indian in 1938 and as a Pakistani in 1948, Mr Alam—and his wife—easily gelled into the social life of Lahore, becoming friends with bureaucrats and notable officials from the elite circle. However, they were still in search of the perfect home. With two children to look after and a majority of the evacuee properties already usurped by the locals as well as the refugees from across the border, the Alams had almost no suitable options left. Seeing how lost they were, one of Mr Alam's tennis buddies, and by then the chief secretary, Akhtar Hussain, offered to give them a tour of vacant properties left unoccupied by nothing else but sheer luck. Unfortunately, their first experience of such a house was simply too much to digest and the Alams turned away, alarmed by what they had seen.

'Janno—ahem, my grandmother—tells me that the people who were sitting there didn't even know how to use electricity. They were pushing a stick towards the fan when they walked in, trying to twirl it for a wave of air. And that wasn't all. There was rotten food waiting to be served at the dining table—the family that lived there before Partition had probably left in a hurry without finishing their meal.' Horrified by this eerie experience, Mr Alam responded even before Mrs Alam could, telling Akhtar Hussain that they certainly didn't want a house that screamed for its old owners from each corner and every corridor.

The Alams' next stop was more fruitful and they quickly made themselves at home in the house they found in Zaman Park, close to Aitchison College. However, before they could get too cosy, the old owner turned up to inform them that the property was not evacuee property but rather had been taken over by the Indian government during World War II without paying any compensation at all. 'When my grandparents asked him where he had been all this while, he sheepishly told them that he had been waiting for them to complete all the renovations he had been ogling at from the side, so that he wouldn't have to do them himself!'

And so, off were the Alams, homeless once again. It was then that Qurban Ali Khan, the SP and later IG Punjab who would often visit Rafay's grandfather in Delhi before Partition, and who was a witness to Hitler's dog, found the Alams living with Mrs Alam's father. From thereon, the journey to 90 Upper Mall was a case of influential phone calls and site visits. By 1959, the Alams had finally found a home in Lahore. The rest, as they say, was history; a history which was only dug up over forty years later, on 22 April 2000.

'So you and your grandparents never spoke much about the house, or Partition, for that matter?'

'No. I think grandfather and Janno had seen a lot of the madness of Partition, a lot of bloodshed, so it was a painful topic for them. And honestly, I don't think I was even bothered enough to ask. That was their story, not mine. I had never been to India and my only association with it was from what I had read in school or seen on TV, which, of course, wasn't very positive.'

Rafay excuses himself to pour himself some more whisky. He is getting more and more relaxed with each glass, while I sit increasingly alert, two cups of coffee down. I look around and notice the tens of trees surrounding us, many of which must have provided shade and greenery to Martand's family before Partition. His grandmother must have grown up in this very garden, jumping up and down like Rafay's daughter is in the background. The family must have had their evening tea, political discussions and get-togethers right where Rafay and I sit. I am picturing a rosy scene involving Martand's family when Rafay walks back in, half a glass of whisky and ice clinking in his right hand.

'You know, my mother's from America. My father's side migrated from India to Pakistan and then he married an American and so did my *chacha* (paternal uncle). I spent most of my life thinking I must be half-American and don't really belong here. I don't even know Urdu fully and I've spent much of my time studying abroad. So while I was growing up, India was never in the equation. It was more about America and Pakistan, about whose side I was on.'

I smile to myself. For CAP's Oral History Project and then for this book, I have spent the majority of my time with the first and second generations of Pakistanis, those born between the 1920s and 1960s. My research has engrossed me so deeply in the Partition narrative, in association and dissociation with the 'other', that for a while I had forgotten the issues that perturb my generation. Many people from the Pakistani upper-middle-class now have Canadian, British or

American citizenship. Others spend years studying abroad, returning only for short visits. And those who do move back, at times come betrothed to *gori* (white) women—far more socially acceptable than returning with a foreign husband, which would instantly spark the reaction: *'Haye Allah tou tumhare bachey musalmaan nahi honge? Tobah tobah.'* (Oh God, so your children will be non-Muslims. Oh my God, forgive us for such a sin.) For these people, what matters are the issues they face in asserting their Pakistani or non-Pakistani selves. Many of them live half their lives in America or Europe and the other half in Pakistan. They don't know which side they belong to more, which side to choose over the other. Here the confusion isn't between India and Pakistan as it is for Shireen (Chapter Four) or Tina (Chapter Three), who consider themselves daughters of both lands; it's between the dual nationalities that they hold voluntarily.

My own cousin, who is American-born and studies at the prestigious Lahore Grammar School, once called me amid the height of anti-American sentiment in Pakistan post the launch of the American War on Terror. She said she was being subjected to discrimination, and wanted my advice:

'My class fellows tell me I'm going to go to hell because I'm American and the Americans are responsible for the murder of innocent Pakistanis.'

'But you're not American, Natasha. Both your parents are Pakistani!'

'But I was born there and I have an American passport.'

'So?'

'They say I can never be a Pakistani and that I should go back to America. What should I do?'

Natasha was in the sixth standard at that time. Today, in

the thirteenth standard, she faces the same dilemma. Does wearing jeans make her American? Does she want to be a Pakistani? Can she be either, just American or Pakistani, or is she both? I don't think she has given India or Batala, from where both of our fathers migrated, much consideration. It is not her concern, she has another identity altogether to deal with.

Dealing with this sort of an identity crisis meant that for years Rafay never gave India a second thought. The fact that his family had a past across the border held little relevance for him. Partition and the Indo-Pak divide seemed too distant for it to matter. As I pour myself some more coffee, I ask Rafay when and how this changed; when did the indifference transform into a quest for discovering his past. When did he become so interested in his heritage that today he grabs the first chance he gets to speak about his history, about the story of 90 Upper Mall? Was this all after the April of 2000?

'Well, I met Martand in college in London. He was an Indian studying architecture and I was a Pakistani enrolled in law school. We had been houseguests at the same houses in London a couple of times so we vaguely knew the same bunch of people. When we started to share space in the William Goodenough facility, we got along like a house on fire. Martand had a great sense of humour, and my wife—then girlfriend— Ayesha and I instantly clicked with him and we became great friends. One day his father, Mr Romi, was in town and came to our dorm. Interestingly, my aunt, Salima Hashmi, was also visiting. It turned out that it was Romi's family that Salima aunty had met earlier in India. Martand must have been talking to his dad about a friend from Lahore and they made the connection that my house was his great-grandfather's home before Partition. But for the longest time we just joked about it. Each time we were together we would tell this story and Martand would claim: "I met Rafay and I saw a picture of the house and announced, *yeh mera ghar hai!*" (I declared that he was living in my home!) It was a Bollywoodized, dramatized version of the whole thing! Even today, whenever he gets the chance, he teases me that I live in his house without paying him rent and I retort that I'm a lawyer; even if he sues me I'd get away with it!'

To Rafay, these connections seemed bizarre. Living in 90 Upper Mall, Rafay had never bothered to find out about its past. As the fourth generation living in Pakistan and having no interest in his heritage, he was all of a sudden presented with links that he could not fully understand. What did it mean for him and Martand to be connected in this way? What was its importance? For so many people from the Partition generation or even their children, connecting these dots between their past and present would hold extraordinary weight. Several people I had met in India and Pakistan were ecstatic to hear the name Lahore or Delhi, they were thrilled to be able to ask what had happened to the streets they had lived on, what their homes looked like now. But for Rafay, and perhaps many others in his generation, being so far removed from Partition meant this association only made an entertaining story to tell, an amusing tale to share.

'I visited India for the first time after I met Martand. Before that I never really cared about going but after college I had made so many Indian friends and being so close to each other, we would keep visiting off and on.' Rafay's first trip was a graduation present from his grandparents. He was meant to travel alone and explore India but the trip turned out to be far more adventurous than he had expected. 'My grandfather's backbone started to give him trouble and we decided to take him to an Ayurvedic centre in the deep dark woods of Kerala. So it was me, fourteen bags, two grandparents and a budget!' He stands up from his chair and lets out an infectious laugh, 'My grandma is a notorious miser. You can't imagine how much I had to haggle with her throughout the trip! I remember she took me to where my grandfather used to work in Bombay, at the ACC building—now a tourist office—behind Churchgate. I wanted to see the Gateway of India from there and she wanted to go home. She told me the best way to get back was the train.' Sitting back in his chair, but still bubbling with excitement, he continues, 'Janno nearly killed herself running for the train! There were a million people already on it and it had started to move when grandma decided to hop on. It was too fast for her to run so she was bouncing up and down and I was running next to her trying to catch her. Somebody pulled her in at the last minute and all she said rather calmly was, "Thank Goodness your grandfather wasn't with us. He wouldn't have let us get on."'

We are both in fits of laughter as we imagine the scene, a nearly eighty-year-old hopping onto the packed Mumbai train. I have seen how crowded these trains are on my trips to India and could never imagine jumping on a moving carriage but Surriya had grown up in Bombay; she was a Bombay girl and she wanted to experience her city in full flow.

'This was all in the July of 2000. Literally, a couple of months after I found out that Martand and I were related in this way, I was in India. But I didn't try to find out anything about our past, nor did I feel the need to go see my grandparents' old home or anything like that. All of that only happened when I sat down to write an article about Martand and my relationship.'

Rafay and his wife Ayesha were at the Jaipur Literary Festival with Martand a few years later when the topic shifted to their intertwined past, a past that made a good story, a powerful ice-breaker whenever they were with new people. 'Martand and I were saying that we would write a book about our story. We were a few drinks down and were laughing that we're probably as good writers as anyone else in the room and we knew the topic of Partition would make all the bucks, regardless of the quality of work. *Yeh tou zaroor chalegi* (It will definitely do well). Meanwhile a woman from *Vogue India*, which had launched recently, was standing next to us asking the author Mohsin Hamid to write an article on Partition and he was complaining that he was too busy. Martand and I overheard this and immediately volunteered to write for her. We said *masla hi koi nahi*—no problem, we'll tell you about Partition, about Hitler's dog.'

It was as Rafay started to put his story down on paper that the amusement with which he used to narrate the story started to crystallize. 'I began to think, *mera jo rishta hai*, my relationship, my experience of Partition, is interesting. This was strange because in my entire life I had never thought I had anything to do with Partition. It had happened years before I was born.'

Although the article was chopped up and heavily edited before being published, the task of writing it had sparked an interest in Rafay to explore his history. For the first time he wanted to know about India, about his heritage. 'Up to when I met Martand, I had little interaction with Indians. I only knew them through history books. And being a lawyer, I'd only get involved in constitutional debates but then I started to write and I started to think about it more and more; about the personal experiences and incidents of Partition, not just the gory details we were made to read in school.'

Rafay first turned towards Mr and Mrs Alam. 'For the first time in all these years we started to speak about their past. I learnt that the last address my grandparents lived in Delhi was 6 Mason Road, close to Connaught Place. You won't believe this but when Martand's family moved from Lahore, they moved into house number 4 on the same street!' This is almost creepy, I think, and if I were slightly superstitious I would be convinced that Martand and Rafay share some deep connection, perhaps from another life altogether. Their grandparents lived in the same house in Lahore, the same street in Delhi and Rafay and Martand had crossed paths so many times in London. All a coincidence? Before I can come up with a supernatural explanation for all of this, Rafay interrupts. 'I guess all these links made me want to know not only my story but Martand's too. I wanted to know what had happened to the Khosla and Natha Singh family at Partition.'

He explains that Martand is the great-grandson of Bawa Natha Singh, the man who had built 90 Upper Mall itself. 'He was an engineer in the irrigation department for the Government of Punjab before Partition and later rose to be the chief engineer of canals. When he retired he bought this property and built a house on it around 1928. It was an interesting piece of land because there was really nothing else here but he built six houses and put them on rent. It was his pension plan,' he smiles. 'This area used to get no water but being a former canal engineer he cut a line from the canal to the house so that water would flow through. Since this place had water all the time after that, it got the name Bawa Park, which it is still referred to as. This house we're sitting in was Bawa Natha Singh's house.'

So what happened to him and his family at Partition? I ask.

'It is said that he and his sons had to flee to India but I don't really know what happened to them. The only reason Martand's grandmother, Bawa Natha Singh's daughter, survived was because she was already married off to a high court judge at the time. The way Partition affected her life was different from what happened to her brothers and the rest of her family.'

Married into the Khosla family, Martand's grandmother—Mrs Khosla—migrated to Indian Punjab with her husband after 1947. By the time Rafay had a chance to talk to her, she was frail and weak, already ninety-seven years old. I ask Rafay what she remembered of Partition and this house and he tells me that she lived here for several years. 'She was married from this house and later, after giving birth, moved back in to nurse two or three of her children in the back porch. The last time she saw the house was in 1947. She left for summer vacations with her husband and children thinking that she would be back in no time but meanwhile Partition happened.'

Mrs Khosla was clueless about the turn her life was about to take. An avid tennis and bridge player, she had won the Gymkhanna Ladies Lawn Tennis Tournament for the third time in a row in 1947. When the club presented her with a trophy, she returned it. 'I want it after I win five times,' she said. She was certain that she would play the next year and the year after that. And so, when she left for Simla in June '47, she didn't think twice about leaving her home or saying goodbye to her family. She would see them again in a few months, she thought.

'It was while she and her husband were in Simla that they began to hear stories about the riots. Then they were told that "you just cannot go back".' Rafay pauses to collect his thoughts, his chin resting on his hand, 'That must have been the time that Bawa Natha Singh's family left the house themselves because no one saw them after that. Apparently, Mr Khosla made one last trip down to Lahore to pick up whatever was in their house. They lived elsewhere so he went to his home first and on the way back stopped here to see the situation but there was no one in the house. That was the last time anyone from Bawa Natha Singh's family saw this place. That is before Martand and his father came to Pakistan, of course.'

'What is it like for them to be here?' I interrupt, eager to know about Mr Romi and his son's journey to their ancestral home. 'Well, I'm sure it's strange for Martand to be here. He never met his great-grandfather or knew much about this house until London but now he has this link with Mall Road, with Bawa Park. He certainly must feel some of that association while he's here. But more than that I think he just really enjoys being in Pakistan. Whenever he comes he eats to his heart's content and has a fantastic time. We throw a party and call all our old friends, Indians and Pakistanis, from college. In fact, he enjoys himself so much that he always ends up sick!' laughs Rafay, 'But for his father, I think, it's a far more overwhelming experience. He was old enough at Partition to remember the colour of the tiles and floor of the house. When he came here he was able to recollect all of that and it was fascinating to see that someone other than my family could also connect with this house like we did.'

'And what about you? What does all of this mean to you now; is it more than a story?' I ask. 'Well there is only so much I can find out about our past. There is a practical limitation. How do I find out about my great-grandparents? I guess I'm not that driven either. Martand and my friendship today is not based on this house. It's just a ridiculous incident; a mindboggling coincidence that has weaved us together in history. I wouldn't say we're friends because of it, we'd still probably be friends, but I suppose the kind of relationship we share would not be the same if it weren't for Partition nor would I have probed my heritage. I would have still found it insignificant but now I know it means something, I know I belong to this soil even if I'm only half-Pakistani. In a way I've realized that I have a relationship with Partition, I share ties with Pakistan's history. It's funny because my Partition story is one which has nothing to do with the violence of that time. It's about how the event uprooted so many lives and how those lives can be reconnected . . .'

Rafay's phone rings and our conversation is interrupted momentarily but his chain of thought hasn't broken when he hangs up. He is more pensive now than I have seen him all evening. 'You know, Anam, I know that I have grown up with a prejudice against India like the rest of us but my personal experience is different and perhaps it's time that we use such stories to rival the hostile discourse that exists now.' I nod but I'm not sure if I fully understand. How do we do that? I ask. 'The violence happened so long ago. We need to let the wounds heal so that it's these connections that emerge more than anything else. There is no reason for people my age—we are the first or second generation of people who have no first-hand experience of Partition—no reason why somebody twelve years old in India or Pakistan should feel hatred for the other apart from what they've read or heard, which is often a biased opinion. If we could only find and share the stories of Indians and Pakistanis who were connected through or after Partition, then as time passes one would understand that animosity shouldn't drive the narrative. It should be learning and connecting or reconnecting.'

Finishing off what is probably more of ice water than whisky, he adds, 'I am proud of Martand and my story. It's a Partition story as much as anyone else's is. Just because it's not a story of violence doesn't mean that it isn't a Partition story, does it?'

What a powerful thought, I think, as we say goodbye and I walk towards my car. Could such stories really start to connect the disconnect of the past sixty-seven years? How many more Martands and Rafays are out there? What if it were these stories that were taught to our children who are at a greater distance from Partition than even Rafay and Martand are? What if it was this narrative that was celebrated and promoted in society, a narrative of friendships and bonds rather than division and enmity? What kind of Indians and Pakistanis, what kind of humans would they grow up to be?

chapter twelve

CLOSING A CHAPTER, STARTING ANOTHER

SHIRAZ

It's about 11.30 in the morning and the 9th of Muharram, according to the Islamic calendar. Muharram marks one of the most sacred months for Muslims. Each year, during this month, Pakistanis are permitted two holidays to mark Ashura, the day of mourning in Shiite Islam. Ashura, which falls on the 10th of Muharram, marks the date when the Prophet's grandson, Hazrat Hussain, was martyred in the Battle of Karbala in 680 CE. Regardless of which religious sect one belongs to, Ashura is considered a sacred day for Muslims and is commemorated all around the Muslim world. As I write this in November 2012, however, Ashura is being commemorated by banning pillion-riding and mobile networks in Pakistan. This is the fourth time in the past four months that Pakistanis are being subjected to this. The interior minister of the ruling Pakistan People's Party, Rehman Malik, insists that mobile phones and pillion-riding facilitate attacks and bomb blasts. While phones can be used to detonate bombs, many attacks that take place across the country are conducted on bikes, often with the passenger seated at the back responsible for shooting while the one in front gears for escape. In order to make the citizens feel more secure, the government now suspends cellular services and pillion riding each time it anticipates unrest in the cities. The first time I recall such a ban in recent times was during Eid-ul-Fitr in August 2012, followed by the national holiday to protest against the movie, *The Innocence of Muslims*. The movie sparked a strong backlash among the Muslim community, which found the depiction of the Prophet (Peace be upon him) sacriligeous and deeply offensive. The Pakistani government declared a national holiday to carry out peaceful protests and declared the day as the Day of Love for the Prophet (Peace be upon him). However, the protests remained nowhere near peaceful and violence rippled through multiple cities despite the bans. Nonetheless, today similar instructions have been implemented once again in hopes of preventing any conflict between the Shia and Sunni sects. The tension between the communities, which dates back to right after Prophet Muhammad's (Peace be upon him) death, has resulted in many ferocious attacks over the years. On Ashura, the threat of attacks is heightened, with hardline Sunni extremists often targeting Shias throughout the country. Mobile networks and pillion-riding is to remain banned in most parts of Pakistan for two days to minimize the risk. A certain respite may be allowed by activating cellular networks late at night when the government feels the chances of attacks are less.

My mother and Haroon advise me to cancel my interviews; they expect trouble between Shias and Sunnis in Lahore. I have to admit that I also have my doubts leaving my house this morning, especially with no way to reach my family and friends in case of any disturbance. It is only when I reach Gloria Jean's, a popular coffee shop in DHA Society (Defence Housing Authority), that I begin to relax. No bombs have gone off on the way and Defence is a safe area. I reassure myself that I should be alright, at least for the next few hours, and that I probably made the right decision in venturing out.

I take a corner seat and realize that I have reached earlier than expected due to the lack of traffic on the roads. There is no sign of Shiraz (the name has been changed to protect his identity), the man I have come to meet. Without any way to reach him, I decide to order some coffee for myself and hope that he shows up in the next few minutes so that my day doesn't go waste.

Shiraz walks into the basement of Gloria Jean's café at about noon. He is just a few minutes late and can almost be considered punctual by Pakistani standards. I have only spoken to him over the phone before this and had worried how we would recognize each other. However, the usually bustling coffee shop is rather quiet today. Most people have opted to stay indoors. Apart from me, there is only one other couple snuggling in a corner. Shiraz and I are able to instantly place one another.

Introduced through a friend for the purpose of this book, I had been told that Shiraz had spent a semester studying in India. He had gone to study at the Management Development Institute in Gurgaon as part of a semester abroad programme in 2011. Forty students were selected from Shiraz's university, LUMS (Lahore University of Management Sciences) to spend three months abroad and while most of the students chose to study in Europe and were preparing for an experience of a lifetime, Shiraz had opted to cross the border to study in India. I had found that strange and wanted to know more. That was how we came to meet today.

'My first priority had always been India. One can go to Europe any day but living in India for three-odd months, and that too as a student, is not an experience many get. I wanted to get to know the country.' Not many people in India or Pakistan that I have come across express the desire to get to 'know the other'. Most are quick to judge, they do not need further knowledge to reiterate what they already know through media channels and hearsay. I am therefore taken aback by Shiraz and wonder if he is more mature than even our seasoned politicians, or if there is another reason for this quest of knowledge.

While not denying the former, in the next few minutes it becomes clear that Shiraz did have his own reasons to go to India, to voluntarily spend months in an antagonistic state. 'My father migrated from Bhagalpur, Bihar, at Partition so I was always keen to see what India was all about.' Did he encourage you to cross the border? I ask him. Did he share fond stories of the pre-Partition years? But he tells me that his father passed away many years before; he wasn't alive to see his son go to his birthplace.

'My father had me when he was much older. He died when I was just a child and with him, the link to my ancestral home also died . . . but some of his stories from his childhood used to still ring loudly in my ears. I wanted to travel through my father's memories; I wanted to see the life he had left behind. I couldn't go to Bihar because I knew no one there; no addresses, nothing. Delhi was simply the next best option. I thought at least I can stand in my father's land, if not his city. It was my way of connecting with him.'

I request Shiraz to tell me some of the anecdotes his father had shared with him. 'My father studied at the Dhaka Medical College and was ten or fifteen years old when Partition happened. I was very young when I lost him but I remember he used to tell us of the house he grew up in in Bhagalpur, Bihar, as a child and the places around it. His sister continued to go back to India for many years even after Partition, but because my father had joined the Pakistan Army, he wasn't ever able to visit.' Defending his country had prevented Shiraz's father from revisiting his past. Serving on the frontline of Kashmir in both the 1965 and 1971 wars, Shiraz tells me that his father always prioritized his country over the relatives or connections he had on the other side. Yet, like many other soldiers posted on the border, he also often spent evenings with his Indian counterparts, laughing and singing songs. He would narrate stories of easily crossing over into Amritsar before the first war to see movies. Occasionally, he would also voice his desire to visit Bihar after retirement. 'Even if my home isn't there, at least I can see my neighbourhood. Maybe I can meet my old friends,' he would say. Unfortunately, death came too early and the wish remained unfulfilled. Today, Shiraz only has vague memories of his conversations with his father. With his death, the family lost their connection with their paternal side. The recollections have begun to fade away, turning into the dust of their beholder's grave.

'I think in a way the link with our heritage was snapped off around the 1971 war, even before I was born. After the Partition of 1947 my father was still able to maintain an association with his culture. He was posted in East Pakistan for several years where he had earlier studied and felt at home. He knew the language; in fact, he loved it. Even until his death, whenever a

Bengali programme would come on TV, he would enjoy translating it for us.' But when the 1971 war broke out and Shiraz's father was made to fight the Bengalis as part of the Pakistan Army mission, he was destroyed.

'He didn't only lose a part of his country, but also his culture. It was really difficult for him. I remember he would always say that by the 1960s the hostility between East and West Pakistan had become unbearable for him. One day while he was in the officers' mess, the Bengalis threw out his luggage on the road and told him to leave because they felt he was a West Pakistani imposing himself on them. That animosity was very difficult for him to bear because though he was born and brought up in Bihar, he had gone to school for some years in Dhaka. The city had carved a special place in his heart. All of a sudden he was disowned and forced to flee. Twice in two decades he had been told to leave his home because Partition had happened.

'I always wish I had been frank with my father and had asked him more about his past but I missed that chance. He always tried to project the tough military-man image at home and it used to scare me as a child. I never openly asked him about what his life used to be like, about how he made sense of that loss.'

We have already started to lose the Partition generation. All we are left with are assumptions, faint recollections, remorse and dwindling connections. That is the burden that the succeeding generations of Pakistan and India will have to bear; for now and forever, we will have to do guesswork. I can only surmise what Shiraz's father may or may not have gone through during the two Partitions; what he may have lost and what had stayed with him till his last breath are only for him to tell.

With his bags packed, Shiraz caught the PTDC (Pakistan Tourism Development Corporation) bus from Lahore to the Wagah border, ready to discover what travelling across the 'big line' felt like. The journey, as he was about to find out, was going to be far bumpier than the smooth sailing to and back from the Pakistani side of the border when he would go see the parade as a child. Crossing over came with its own rattling jolts. 'I had all the papers with me and thought I wouldn't face any problems but the officials, on both the Pakistani and Indian side, made me open my luggage several times. Then they kept inquiring why I was going to India. They weren't satisfied with my answers. Fortunately, the letter from my university eventually worked.'

As the bus finally drove through the Indian gate, amidst the sirens of the VIP escorting vans and a sign that read, 'Welcome to the largest democracy in the world,' Shiraz leaned back in his seat and slowly started to soak in the scenery; the green fields, different car models, wine shops and Vodafone ads surrounding him amongst the pink, yellow and blue turbans of the sardars walking on the streets. 'We crossed Panipat, Jalandhar, places that I had read about in history books, seen in movies. A lot of it looked like Pakistan but then you'd see mandirs and gurdwaras crop up at different intervals that you wouldn't see at home. That was the reality check, a reminder that I was in India.'

The Management Development Institute at Gurgaon had housed Pakistani students before. A special welcome party had been arranged for exchange students; the faculty exhausted all hospitality in making Shiraz feel welcomed. With so many new faces on campus, Shiraz did not stick out. All new students, both local and foreign, were on their best behaviour; they all wanted to fit in and make friends. Within days Shiraz gelled with them; like Owais (Chapter Nine), he quickly came to see how similar they were to his friends back home. It is these friendships that he made in those initial few weeks that continue to pull him towards India; that make him want to go back and visit. I am not surprised to hear this; everyone I have conversed with who has travelled to India has come back with new friends, with intimate ties that connect them even years later. I ask him if, in the middle of these fresh relationships and bonds, he was able to trace his ancestral roots. Was he able to find the connection with Bihar that he was searching for? Had his visit served its purpose?

'Well, not quite. I did meet many Biharis during my stay and the first thing I would tell them was that my father was from Bihar. I would ask them if they knew about Bhagalpur, my father's ancestral city. But most of them had moved to Delhi or other cities when they were very young. They weren't able to tell me much. I began to realize that it wasn't so simple; I couldn't wake up one morning and recover my heritage. It wasn't that easy.' The thirst to discover his past was unlikely to be quenched on this trip.

'I think in the first month I accepted the fact that I wasn't going to be able to revive the link with my family's past. What was I even supposed to ask for? I barely knew anything myself. Plus I didn't even have the visa to go to nearby cities so it just wasn't possible to travel to Bihar. Living in Gurgaon, how much could I find out? I realized how naïve I had been before coming.'

Resigned to his situation, Shiraz decided to discover the India that he could reach out to. It may not have been his father's India but it was still a country he wanted to explore. 'The Indians were very hospitable and took me around to see Delhi. Whenever I would feel homesick they would treat me to mutton and chicken dishes . . . They even took me to Jamia Masjid! I offered my prayers there and it felt like I was at home.'

Hearing that Shiraz was from Lahore, one of the professors at the college, Neelu, called him over to her house for dinner. 'Her father had migrated from Lahore so she was very keen to hear about it. She kept asking me what Mall Road looked like now, whether I had seen Government College. She had never been to Pakistan but said her father spoke about Lahore a lot.' Wistful about her father's past life, she had asked Shiraz to bring back pictures of Mall Road for her. When he said he would, she promised to make him home-cooked meals in return. 'She was really nice and very open-minded too. She made us talk to her son who held typical misconceptions about Pakistan; he was just twelve or thirteen years old and thought that all Pakistanis were terrorists. In fact, a lot of people I came across, especially those from Mumbai, were convinced that we were fanatics, that our women were confined behind the doors and only wore *burqas*. When I would show them pictures of Pakistani models they would be so impressed!' he lets out a laugh but a moment later becomes pensive. 'You know, I think it's very important to clear out these fallacies. We have them about the Indians and they have them about us. I didn't meet too many people so I couldn't change their overall opinion but I tried to make a small effort; I asked them to come to Pakistan, to explore Lahore. That is the only way we will stop fighting with each other.'

I ask him if during his stay he ever faced any animosity.

Was he at any point made to feel unwelcome? Did the misconceptions lead to hostile interactions with the Indians? He nods uncomfortably. 'A few times I got into heated arguments with some students. I remember once this boy Abhishek kept insisting that Pakistan should leave Kashmir to India. He said we had governance issues in the provinces and cities we already had, that we should let Kashmir be taken care of by the Indians. I felt provoked and in anger retorted that India should stop infringing upon our sovereignty; they should stop building dams on our rivers. The situation got out of hand and a few people from Mumbai who were sitting nearby got involved. The attacks were still fresh in their minds and they started telling me to go back home, that there was no space for fundamentalists in India.'

Fortunately, a teacher stepped in at the right moment and diverted a potentially serious fight between the Pakistani and Indian students, who were standing with their collars up and fists charged. But I wonder if such bitter incidents affected the way Shiraz sees India today. He had walked in voluntarily; he may have been apprehensive but he was also intrigued to explore his father's birthplace, curious to see what India was all about. Did these encounters make him inimical to the neighbour?

'I don't think I ever regretted going there. In fact, I'm really happy I made that decision. I was very inquisitive about India, I wanted to see what it was like and I got to do that. Looking back I can understand why some Indians didn't like having me in their country; they hear terrible news about us every day and since most of them never come across ordinary Pakistanis, that image sticks with them. I guess they can't be blamed.' He reaches for his coffee as he says this; finishing off the last sip he begins to circle the rim with the edge of his thumb and looks at me. 'I returned with an understanding that in different times in our history, India and Pakistan have both wronged each other but the youth don't have anything to do with that. We also don't have the mandate to address these issues so what's the point of politicizing common relationships? I don't need to fight over Kashmir; that's not my job. For me India is a place with a lot of friends and many memories. That's my only connection with it.'

'And what about your connection with Bihar?' I ask him. 'What about your ancestral links?'

'Well, honestly, I don't think I'll ever go to Bihar. I guess that connection really died with my father,' he sighs. 'I don't know anyone in Bihar now. I don't know what I would do even if I went there. I guess it's really history. My friends are in Delhi; that is the place I have an association with. That's where I would like to go back.'

For a moment I am shocked to hear this. The roots that had pulled Shiraz towards India had begun to weaken. Instead of deepening his ties with his ancestry, Shiraz had closed that chapter of his life. But then I realize that his sentiments are not an anomaly. He is a reflection of myself and the numerous other people from our generation. I have also been to India thrice over the last year; I also share roots across the border. But when I think of India today, do I think of Batala or Delhi and Mumbai, cities where I have built my own relationships, from where I have my own experiences. How important is the Batala of my *dadi* to me? Would I ever go back? Would I ever make the effort? And if I did, what would I look for? Who would I ask for? I have no addresses, no familiar faces to locate.

Too many people from our generation are disconnected from their past. Some, like Owais (Chapter Nine), come across their roots in passing conversations. Others through photo albums or old letters they find when cleaning out their late parents' cupboards. But regardless of the scraps we find, we are unable to speak to our elders about their stories and experiences, about their roots and culture. In my case as well as the cases of Shiraz and Owais, the sources have already departed to another world before we can even begin to understand what heritage means. The details and directions have faded away. The desire to go is waning too. The new generations have moved on and made their own connections with India . . . For Shiraz and Owais it is these bonds that are likely to sustain the divide in between . . .

PART IV

REDEFINING PARTITION

'BHARAT SE RISHTA KYA?'

chapter thirteen

A DELHI THAT WAS
ONLY THEIRS

MANSOOR AHMAD

Grey clouds have cast a shadow above me as I make my way to interview Mansoor Ahmad, a distinguished Pakistani diplomat. It is 13 July and by now the monsoon should have engulfed Lahore but we are still waiting for the first shower of rain.

The car stops outside a big black gate in the elite society of Model Town. The guard asks me to introduce myself and then opens it. As I drive in I am welcomed by vast amounts of greenery. One of Mansoor's servants is resting under a banyan tree to seek refuge from the humidity that usually takes over the city at the onset of the rains. As he hears the car drive in, he turns sideways on his charpoy with one of his elbows resting on the pillow beneath him, his head propped up on his hand. For a few seconds he watches in amusement as a girl drives past him but then returns to his old posture. In ordinary circumstances he would have continued to glare as people often do on the streets when they see a woman driving. But the scorching afternoon has made the boy lazy. He slumps his head back in exhaustion, allowing the tree to shade him from each corner. Its large leathery leaves have a brownish-red tinge to them; they are his only source of shade.

A smaller gate separates this unruly garden from the main entrance. Inside, a modern brick house and two fancy cars greet me. Mansoor Ahmad is leaning against one in a light grey suit, his shoulders back and his hands resting in his pockets. Holding the recording kit in one hand I lock the car and walk up to him, slightly nervous about conducting an interview with such a seasoned bureaucrat. But his face breaks into a warm smile as he receives me and any initial hesitation melts away. I tell him that I love his garden and he responds in English, his accent refined, 'Oh yes, we have quite a jungle out there. Not sure if you can call it a garden but it's lovely indeed!'

Swinging open the wooden door, he guides me into a large drawing room. Huge windows encircle the seating area and despite the dark clouds, thin rays of light creep in. Asking his cook to make two glasses of lemonade, he tells me to make myself comfortable. I take this opportunity to look around and spot an enormous library at one end. Paintings and wall hangings surround us from the other. It seems like the house has been set up with a lot of dedication.

I ask Mansoor how long he has lived here. Many people who have homes in Model Town have resided there for several years. The society has a history of its own. 'Oh, this house is relatively new but my connection with Model Town goes back to the 1930s.' I am happy to hear this and decide to put away my questionnaire for a while. Model Town was a Hindu-dominated area before Partition. If Mansoor's relationship with it dates back to the early 1900s then he must have lived amongst many Hindus. I want to hear more about that time.

The Model Town I have grown up seeing has always had only Muslim residences. Many of my own relatives live there, their houses newly renovated and classy; the past well-covered with bright paint and polished furniture.

'Most of the people who lived here were judges, doctors, engineers or professors. My father was a professor at Government College and so we also moved here. We lived at House Number 98 E. It was a four *kanal* (half-an-acre) house with two gates and many servants!' he says proudly. 'Model Town was absolutely delightful then. It was calm, sparsely populated, peaceful.'

I notice that as he speaks about those days the crispness in his voice has given way to a softer tone. 'You know, despite all that is said today, I don't recall any animosity between Muslims and Hindus, even though this was a Hindu-dominated area. It was G block where most of the Muslims lived, but here in E block it was 90 per cent Hindus and yet my father chose to live here because he didn't anticipate any problems. We lived with them, went to school with them. We were friends, cordial, if nothing else. I used to study in St. Anthony's High School and there too there were hardly any Muslims. Most of our friends were Hindus; there were a few Sikhs too. Things were always alright between us, at least up to Partition,' he pauses, his expression sombre, 'But we all really lost it then . . .'

I can feel our conversation head towards 1947, for he knows I am here to converse with him about it, but I am not quite ready to speak about Partition as yet. I know those memories will be as excruciating for him as they have been for the other people I have spoken to. Refugee camps, threat of attacks, altered life plans and ruptured families come to my mind. I am sure Mansoor has a story of his own to share. But before we get there I want to know more about his life prior to this madness. I want to know about St. Anthony's, one of the oldest schools in Pakistan.

'It was wonderful,' he says. 'The education was top-notch. Our teachers were either Anglo-Indians or Irish brothers. If you come from Regal Chowk, you will see a brick building next to the church; that was my school.' The tender smile returns to his face as he recalls the tall structure standing in the middle of Lawrence Road. St. Anthony's is responsible for educating some of the leading bureaucrats, army officials, politicians and sportsmen of Pakistan. Built in the late 1800s, the school is a part of the Roman Catholic Archdiocese of Lahore and is renowned for its splendid architecture and academic achievements. As an alumnus, Mansoor is proud to speak about his school.

'It didn't have grounds like Aitchison College or Central Model School but we had ample space at the front and back for hockey and boxing. It was here that I built some of my strongest friendships.' Since the school was heavily populated with Hindus and a number of Sikhs, Mansoor's friends were largely from these communities. As children the religious distinctions that were going to distance them in the near future did not make any sense. They all liked to play the same games, they all ran away from studies; everyone wanted to eat ice creams and *chaat* and each one of them was thrilled at the prospect of Eid and Diwali holidays. To these youngsters, it was these things that mattered. Yes, they all practised their faiths, their parents made sure of it. But when it came to cramming before examinations or representing their school in various tournaments, the Hindus, Sikhs and Muslims always came together. After all, they lived next to each other; they studied together in every class. How far apart or different could two fourteen-year-olds be? The categories of faith failed to distinguish between Hindu happiness and Muslim pleasure, Islamic grief and non-Islamic misery.

'We would always play together in the evenings in front of our houses and one of the parents would call us in for food. I ate many meals with my neighbours, most of whom were Hindu but we never thought in those terms back then. We would quickly gobble down whatever was there on our plate and then run out to play again. There was no hatred between us at this time and I think that was because of the way our school was organized. Its sole objective was to impart education; politics and religion were strictly off boundaries.'

I ask Mansoor if this friendly momentum was maintained as the Pakistan movement gained fervour and Partition threatened to become a reality. Did the conditions outside school, which were becoming increasingly volatile, affect the friendships which were flourishing inside? 'Well it's not as if we were oblivious,' he says. 'We knew the Muslims were fighting for a separate homeland; in fact, my own father was a staunch Muslim League supporter so we were certainly well aware of the circumstances. Even in school, sometimes, we students would joke around. The Muslims would pass comments on Gandhi and the Hindus would retort with remarks about Jinnah. But it was all in good humour. In fact, just up to the summer of 1947, even up to July, everything was normal, our relations healthy.'

Mansoor tells me that it was the month of Ramadan and the Muslims, Hindus and Sikhs were getting ready to prepare for Eid. This was common, he says. In the tightly-knit community of Lahore, everyone would participate in each other's festivals. Sweets would be distributed, new clothes would be made. Children would enthusiastically put up lights and decorations, unable to contain their excitement for the coming days. *Melas* would be organized, swings and food stalls the highlight. The Hindus, who owned most of the *mithai* shops, would stack up hundreds of boxes, forming a pyramid of colourful delights. Each day customers would flutter around them, buying kilos' worth of sweets.

'We were looking forward to Eid when all hell broke loose. I don't know what happened but it was within those next few days that we came to slitting each other's throats. That is something I still cannot reconcile with. What happened to us?' His voice echoes in the room. A strange heaviness takes over our surroundings. Outside, the first splash of monsoon rain pours down, slamming against the windows. The air inside the room becomes moist, our skins cold and sticky.

From the festive mood to cut-throat rivalry and revenge, the drastic turn of events do not make any sense to Mansoor even today. To abruptly slash off relationships, to tear apart friendships overnight cannot be rationalized. To kill one's own people is even more horrifying; it is absolutely inconceivable. I want to know what happened to his Hindu and Sikh class fellows as the tensions escalated and the communities collided head on. Did they get to say their goodbyes?

From the window behind him I can see the rain falling heavily, feeding the starved trees that have been begging for its arrival. The ivy crawling up the windows has become greener, the grass stands erect, rejuvenated by the blinding rain drops; the harsh days are over, it can dance in the breeze, it can shower in the rain. But only for a few moments; before Mansoor responds, the rain has already deserted us, gone as quickly as it came. The sun makes its way through the clouds, shoving and pushing until it has attained its central position once again. The heat this time is of a different kind; it pierces, baking the skin, the leaves, the flowers, and the grass, everything it finds beneath.

'There was no change, no transition,' Mansoor says, his voice loud against the silence that has followed the rain.'It was sudden; a complete cut-off. We said goodbye to each other before the summer vacations, taking it for granted that we would meet after a few weeks, and then everything went haywire. Muslims were pouring in from East Punjab and the massacre of Sikhs and Hindus in Rawalpindi had led to riots in Lahore. The peaceful multicultural city was nowhere to be seen. It had been ravaged with the vultures that were attacking its core. Looting, killings, rape . . . it was everywhere.'

Several accounts of Partition that I have come across say that it was the riots in Rawalpindi in the March of 1947 that triggered off other events. Ishtiaq Ahmed, author of *The Punjab Bloodied, Partitioned and Cleansed* (OUP Pakistan 2012), writes in a newspaper article that the most critical rioting took place in Pindi:

'On March 5, Sikh-Hindu agitators began shouting anti-Pakistan slogans and were challenged by Muslims. Firearms, stabbings and arson were employed by both sides. Initially, the non-Muslims felt they had been successful in driving off Muslims from the streets of Rawalpindi. In the evening of March 6, however, the direction of violence changed from the city to the villages in the district. Suddenly armed Muslims in the thousands began to raid Sikh villages. Neighbouring villages in the Attock and Jhelum districts were also surrounded. In some places the Sikhs fought back, but on the whole the conflict was one-sided . . . Government statistics claim 2,000 dead, but Sikhs say that as many as 7,000 lost their lives . . . In some places nearly the whole Sikh and Hindu populations were wiped out. However, the deaths included the Sikhs killing their own women and children rather than letting them fall in the hands of Muslim marauders.'[8]

Mansoor, a young school boy, felt the repercussions first-hand.

'I once saw people get butchered right outside my house. I was a young boy then, playing in my garden, when the commotion outside caught my attention. When I went out I saw a family of four lying scattered on the road, covered in blood. It was extremely disturbing, especially as a child, to see this. It didn't make sense . . .

'But, you know, the strange part is that even when these riots were taking place and the violence was rampant, there was hope that things would go back to normal; none of us thought that this could be permanent,' he sighs as he allows me to document the last feeble hope that he had held. His eyes are moist by now. They have witnessed the implications of Partition, they have been part of the history of the subcontinent; they were bystanders to the mayhem that was caused.

'My own family was such a strong follower of the Muslim League. We supported the creation of Pakistan; my elders had fought for it. But any happiness we felt on 14 August was buried by these sad events. No one thought Pakistan meant

---

[8]Ahmed, Ishtiaq, 'A Bloody March in 1947', *The News*, 18 August 2007.

this . . . it was supposed to be paradise on earth but the day its creation was announced, Lahore became a living hell. Refugees were coming into Lahore in deplorable conditions, tents and camps were set up but nothing was enough. They were too many. Where were we to put them?'

Mansoor feels that Partition wrought permanent psychological modifications in society. The people they had grown up amongst were being thrown out of their houses. Shahalmi, the Hindu-Sikh neighbourhood, was up in flames. From the opposite end, blood-strewn trains and butchered bodies were coming in. The city in which everyone knew everyone was struck with a strange fate. Those who had lived there for centuries were nowhere to be seen. Instead, Lahore had to host millions who had no connection with the city, but who were compelled to call it the only home they had been left with. The city had a new face, the character of its people altered.

But while Hindus, Muslims and Sikhs were at each other's throats, raping women and butchering children, the same people were also reaching forward to seek help, to give each other the only support that was possible in such chaos. Camps were set in the renowned DAV college to give shelter to the thousands of Hindus and Sikhs who were made homeless overnight. The roof that had been snatched from over their heads had been replaced by the open sky and some flimsy bedsheets; but that was a luxury in its own right. At night trucks would come to transport these victims of Partition to their new home, India. There was no longer any space for them in Lahore. But in the hearts of the people they had lived with for generations, they continued to hold a special place. They were their friends, neighbours, brothers.

Muslims came forward to give them food, to give them
security from the turmoil outside. Pushing them safely into
the trucks, they asked them to promise that they would write
to them as soon as they reached the other side; that they would
come back as soon as the conditions improved.

At this time Mansoor was still too young to be actively
involved. But over the years and much after the mania of
Partition had subsided, he tried to locate his childhood friends.
This wasn't an easy task but as a diplomat with many
connections he was able to identify a few of his friends from
St. Anthony's. Later, he tells me, a number of them even came
to Lahore for their reunion. Through the years he has been in
constant touch with them, exchanging letters and at times
phone calls to find out how they are doing, to remain a small
part of their lives. After all, childhood friends are not meant to
be forgotten. They share the intimate days of the past, of
innocence and naïve aspirations.

Mansoor has been to India once too. Unfortunately, he
was unable to meet these friends on this trip; it was a sudden
trip, and his wife's request to act as complete tourists in a city
she wished to discover meant that the old boys' gathering
would have to be pushed to another date. But despite their
best attempts to act as visitors who knew no one in a country
where Mansoor had many friends, his wife and him were
terribly unsuccessful.

Delhi is home to countless Lahoris. Many of the auto-
drivers, shopkeepers and leading businessmen that I have
spoken to over my trips have their roots in Lahore. It is a city
of migrants; in many ways like Karachi which houses mohajirs
from all over India. During their short stay, Mansoor and his
wife came across several such people; they may not have been

his friends from his youth but like them these people had also left their homes and hearts behind on the Pakistani side of the border. Their assets had been swallowed in the moulding landscape of Lahore but their memories and association with the city could not be buried in the era that had passed them by.

'We met many Hindus, many of whom were from Lahore itself, and I can't tell you how friendly they were. We stayed at Karol Bagh, which is famous for its shops, especially the tailoring ones. The shopkeepers got so excited when they heard we were from Lahore. One of them even told me that he used to run a shop on McLeod Road before Partition.'

McLeod Road, where my father's family moved at Partition, is located near the popular Lakshmi Chowk and was once full of Hindus. The area was famous for its restaurants and later, movie halls. People would come spend their evenings on the streets, eating at the roadside hotels amid the hustle and bustle of the commercial area. Later, many Muslims settled there, taking over the evacuee properties left by the Hindus. My own father's family had done the same.

'Everyone I met there who was from Lahore spoke so fondly of it. They would get tears in their eyes and ask me what it looked like now. What had happened to so and so place, if I knew about so and so family. Even the guesthouse we stayed at was run by a Hindu who had briefly lived in and got married in Lahore and he told us about his house. It was such a coincidence that I actually knew the Muslim family that lived there now. When he heard this he almost began to cry and from that day there was no end to his hospitality. He even told his servant, *"Bhai, in ke liye Urdu channel lagao."* (Put on some Urdu channel for them!)'

Mansoor tells me the guesthouse owner spoke fluent Urdu

and told him how lovely it was to interact with someone from Lahore. He said he often thought about it; Lahore was a city which didn't leave one easily. Mansoor's response was equally warm, he was glad to meet people like him in India. As he says, it made him realize what a deep connection Indians and Pakistanis have, even all this time later. 'For so many people in Delhi, Lahore is home and for so many people in Karachi and Lahore, Delhi is where they spent their childhood, where they grew up. Our paths are tied together in a strange course of history; it is impossible to get away from that.'

But even as he says this, Mansoor knows that this bond only applies to a certain group of people today. The owner's own daughter, who lived at the guesthouse, denied their existence. She was wary of hosting Pakistanis; she did not understand why her father was so friendly with 'them'. She had heard about the terrorist attacks, about the suspicious activities Pakistanis were often involved in. She did not see any point in talking to 'them'.

'For so many Pakistanis and Indians this connection is irrelevant today, in fact, it is often outright rejected.' Mansoor's brows cross in unease as he says this. For a man of his age, for a person who has grown up amongst people who are now considered as the 'other', it is puzzling. Yet he knows it's the truth. He has represented Pakistan for years on international platforms. He has witnessed the growing antagonism between the two counties. He has seen the backlash in Pakistan and India against any rapprochement efforts towards each other. He has read the street banners outside, propagating violence against the infidels of India.

'It is sad that the new generations don't feel this link,' he comments after a while. 'There is so much enmity in them. I find many youngsters these days who loathe the Indians. Even there, there is this ill feeling. The owner's own daughter didn't once ask us what her father's house was like, what Lahore was like, how our trip was, whether we had seen the highlights of the Indian capital . . . I suppose she didn't see any point in talking to us; she was born and raised in Delhi, you see; in a Delhi which could not be shared, a Delhi that was only theirs.'

chapter fourteen

CHILDREN OF ANIMOSITY

ADAN ALI

There were many young people in Pakistan I had personally come across who exemplified what Mansoor (Chapter Thirteen) said: they were hostile to the 'other'. It seemed like not everyone in the younger generation was able to move on from the bitterness of Partition; many were clinging on to the past, albeit a filtered past they had reinterpreted and digested as their own.

One of the main findings of political psychologist Ashis Nandy's research on Partition is that 'those who had actually faced the violence, those who are direct victims, the first generation of victims, those who have been subject to the violence, those who have seen it first-hand, mostly were those who had lesser prejudice and lesser bitterness about their experience than their own children and their grandchildren because they had lived in communities where the other side was the majority . . . they have lived with them and they have very warm memories of that experience. Many of them have said that those were the best days of their lives, whereas the children have a packaged view mostly of those violent days and how the family survived ... so they carry more bitterness, more hostility.'[9]

At first glance, when I came across this study, it had baffled me. Many people from the Partition generation still held on to severe prejudices and bitterness; my grandmother was a case in point, but so were several other Partition survivors I spoke with. On the other hand, people in the younger generation, such as Rafay (Chapter Eleven), Owais (Chapter Nine) and Shiraz (Chapter Twelve), were ready to move on and build new meanings of the 'other'. But as I delved more and more into my work, I began to arrive at findings similar to Nandy's.

One of my colleagues, Mariam, a twenty-two-year-old graduate from the Lahore University of Management Sciences (LUMS), told me she had hated India. She had hated it so much that when her father was posted to Delhi as a defence attaché, she had told him, 'Abba, take us anywhere else in the world, why does it have to be India?' For months, she and her sisters dwelled in this misery. Her younger sister, Maham, would cry her eyes out every night. She would say, *'Hum India kyun ja rahe hain? Udhar tou sarey kafir hotey hain . . . woh tou achey nai hotey.'* (Why are we going to India? Only infidels live there. They aren't good people.) Maham was of a tender age of five.

Later, when they moved there, Mariam tells me an Indian neighbour would often visit. 'He was a Hindu who migrated from Mianwali at Partition. When he found out that we had moved to Delhi, he would visit us all the time! My *dada* (paternal

9'A Psychological Study of India's Partition', *Sanhati*, 21 March 2009, http://sanhati.com/articles/1299/.

grandfather), who was also from Mianwali and had come to India with us, would sit every evening describing the city and his house to the neighbour and he would always leave our place teary-eyed, only to return the next day to hear the same stories over and over again ... I didn't understand why this neighbour would come over all the time ... I used to think it was annoying that this Hindu man was taking up our family time. Why was his home, of sixty years ago, so important to him? It's only now that I understand. After living in India for a few years, I began to let go of that hatred; I became friends with Indians. Today, I can't go back because of my father's military past ... there are just too many security complications to get through ... and that hurts. This man had lived in Mianwali for most of his life ... I don't know how much it must have hurt him to not be able to go back but at the time I just didn't get it. I didn't understand why my *dada* would invite him over and over again.'

Another student I worked with in a school had started crying hysterically when I passed around a picture of a Hindu deity; she was in Class 6, studying in an upper-middle-class school in Lahore that I worked in. When I asked her what happened, she told me her eyes had sinned; that she would now go to hell because of what she had seen. Later that year, when I took a few students with me to India for CAP's Exchange-for-Change programme, one of the Indian schools had received us with garlands and music. The principal had moved forward to place a *tika* on our foreheads. Three of the Pakistani students had begun to cry; they turned and asked me if this meant they had become Hindu. They said they had heard Hindus would forcibly convert Muslims to their religion; was this their fate too?

I wondered whether these children had ever heard the stories I had also only recently come across; about Hindus, Sikhs and Muslims celebrating religious festivals, about Hindus who did not convert but instead saved their elders? I wondered if they knew how many of their great-grandparents had homes across the border, how much they ached to see their friends and neighbours one more time.

And I began to wonder if what Nandy had said could be true; could it be that many in the younger generation were becoming even more resentful, more bitter towards the 'other' as they moved further and further away from the generation who had lived amidst 'them'? Could it be that the same distance, which allowed some people to move on and build fresh relationships and memories with the 'other', was also giving space for old hatreds to be maintained and new animosity to be bred? And if this was the case, why was this happening?

'Afghanistan has Pathans!' 'Iran has oil!' 'China makes everything!' And what about our fourth neighbour, India? I probed, hoping to keep up the momentum in a hall packed with 300 ten-to fourteen-year-olds. It was 2010 and I was at the launch of CAP's Exchange-for-Change programme in an upper-middle-class school in Lahore.

The premise of the programme was that most Indians and Pakistanis spent entire lifetimes without ever communicating with each other. Through a sixteen-month initiative, CAP and its Indian counterpart, Routes2Roots (R2R), hoped to enable people-to-people contact between the two countries. With governments projecting the other as the enemy state and media channels further exacerbating the rivalry through anti-India and anti-Pakistan propaganda, there were many negative stereotypes and misunderstandings breeding in society against the 'other'. The programme wanted to challenge this rhetoric by allowing the youth of both sides to learn about the 'other' through the 'other' itself. The idea was to step away from the politics of the two states and enable a better understanding of the shared past, of lifesyles and cultures across the border.

After a successful pilot project between 2010 and 2012, the Exchange-for-Change programme has scaled tremendously. The programme is ongoing and targets different students and schools in each cycle. So far, it has reached out to 12,000 Pakistani and Indian students in total and has engaged fifty-one schools from Lahore, Karachi, Rawalpindi, Delhi, Mumbai, Chandigarh and Dehradun. It is currently renowned as the largest Track 2 diplomacy initiative between India and Pakistan.

In the pilot project that I was spearheading for CAP, a sustained dialogue was to be initiated among 2,400—and later another 3,500—young students ranging from the ages of ten to fourteen. These were considered to be the formative years, when opinions were in the process of being formed but were not yet too hardline. Ten schools were selected across Lahore, Karachi, Delhi and Mumbai. For over a year, students in all four cities were going to write letters, snap photographs and record oral histories of their grandparents to send across to students they had never met on the other side of the border. And at the end of the project, a handful of students were going to have a chance to visit Lahore and Delhi and meet with the students they had corresponded with.

This time, my question regarding what was special about

India was received with pin-drop silence. Then a few children at the back started to snicker. A small girl nervously raised her hand and in a meek voice asked, 'Shahrukh Khan?' The others began to roll from side to side with laughter. 'He's a Pakistani, stupid! He's Muslim. Muslims can't be Indian,' said one child. Another overconfident student got up from the middle row and declared, 'India has nothing! They will all go to hell!'

Adan, a ten-year-old student of seventh standard, was sitting amongst these children, armed with his own jokes to crack. 'Indians don't cut their hair, Ma'am,' 'They are dirty people,' 'They are cheaters; that's how they won the cricket match!' Though not every child participated in the mockery and many perhaps only did so due to peer pressure, for several initial weeks that I returned to the school, I was received with the same sarcastic expressions, crude comments and empty-handed students. Many of the students told me they hated Indians, that they didn't want to write them any letters. No one in the room had ever been to India and the majority of the students had never met an Indian either. However, the hatred they expressed seemed almost personal, and incredibly powerful.

Certainly, CAP had assumed some resistance on part of the schools and students. We had also expected hate mail. The very goal of the project was to challenge this resistance, to transform it into an openness to dialogue, to cultural exchange. After all, these students have been nurtured in a Pakistan that has fought several wars with India; some whose fathers were in the Pakistan Army would have felt the direct impact of the rivalry across the border. They have also heard about Indian soldiers committing atrocities at the LoC, of harassing Muslims in Indian Kashmir. They have been told, just as I was, that India took away not only Kashmir but also East Pakistan.

Many recent conspiracy theories state that India is behind the terror attacks in Pakistan, that they are funding terrorist outfits so that Pakistan becomes unstable and eventually collapses under its own weight. These theories are becoming increasingly popular, so much so that auto-rickshaws across Lahore publicly carry signs that read, 'Bharat se rishta kya? Nafrat ka, intikam ka.' (What is our relationship with India, but that of hatred and revenge.) Perhaps it was this relationship that the students were emulating and displaying in their classrooms, too. In fact, it wasn't just the students; school administrators and teachers also showed similar, though more subdued, sentiments.

I had toured many schools across Lahore before finding three to work with. Most schools wanted to have nothing to do with an exchange programme that was with India and we had received many rejections. The tagline of the project—'to celebrate similarities and appreciate differences' between India and Pakistan—angered most people. A head administrator of one of the largest upper-middle-class private school networks in Pakistan told me that by suggesting such a programme, I was challenging the Two-Nation Theory. Why would we want children to explore the similarities between the two nations when there was nothing similar in the first place? After all, that was why Pakistan had been created, because we were two separate nations that could no longer live together. She told me the project was a waste of time and I should instead initiate it with China. When I told her the cultures of China and Pakistan were very different, she told me I didn't realize how different those treacherous Indians were from the pure and innocent Pakistanis, and then politely asked me to leave.

Over time and under the fear of their principal, the students began to jot down their thoughts and ideas. Messages started to pour in and while several brilliant letters and poems were composed, giving us a breath of relief, others were tarnished with disgust and scornful remarks. 'India is the worst country on earth,' 'We hope you die,' 'We will never come to India!'

Two years later, I decide to visit Adan at his house to understand some of these sentiments. Adan was not only part of the project but was also one of the twelve students selected to visit India. The trip had taken place in February 2012 and I had noticed how much Adan had changed by this time as compared to my first interaction with him in 2010, when he sat in the front row mocking the exchange and refusing to write any letters. I want to know what his experience has been like, where the changes have come from and what he has learnt from his trip across the border. It is November 2012 by the time I visit him in his house in Phool Nagar, Lahore, and Adan has turned thirteen. He is far more mature now. Sitting in his bedroom, he hesitatingly tells me, 'We were very non-serious when you came to our school. We didn't want to write letters to those Indian students sitting in Mumbai or Delhi. All my classmates, all of us, just thought if they're sitting in India, let them be. Why do we have to talk to them? I think a lot of us were also scared of India; we had heard such bad things about them.'

I ask him to tell me more about what he had thought at that time. 'Well our parents always told us that Sikhs were very bad, that they had tortured millions of Muslims,' he begins, 'And our teachers also said that Indians were arrogant and hostile people. They would say that they don't know how to respect Allah and that they had treated our elders horribly.'

Sitting in Punjab, a province that turned into a bloodbath

because of Muslim-Sikh clashes, I am not surprised to hear this. I prod him to tell me more about what he had heard and he shrugs his shoulders. 'I don't know. I had read a chapter in my Class 5 Urdu book. It said: *Woh bachchon ko talwar se maar diya karte the. Un ke tukre tukre kar diya karte the.* (The Sikhs would slaughter Muslim children with swords. They used to cut them up into tiny pieces), so we thought why should we talk to them? We are good people, they are evil. We would rather tear their letter than write a reply to them.'

Looking almost apologetic, Adan stops to observe my reaction to everything he is saying. Perhaps he is afraid of what I'll think of him and before I can say anything he finds it necessary to defend himself. 'I don't know why I felt so strongly about this because I had never even seen a Sikh in my life but it wasn't just me. Ninety-five per cent of the students were against the Indians and a hundred per cent were against the Sikhs.'

I assure Adan that he can speak openly with me. My own upbringing in Lahore has not been devoid of such opinions; neither would be the teachers who had taught Adan about the big bad Indians. The Sikhs had come and butchered our men, *they* had molested our women. *They* would swipe their swords swiftly across the necks of all Muslims; there was no mercy at *their* hands. A woman I had once spoken to had told me she had seen a Sikh stab a pregnant Muslim woman; lifting her in the air on the edge of his sword he had declared, 'This is the Pakistani flag; this is the fate of your country.' These are the facts that have been drilled into Adan and me and a thousand other children over and over again. Without ever having the chance to meet or even read about a Sikh who did not slay everyone who came before him, what other perspective could one hold of this community? The same image of Hindus resonates among children and adults, boys and girls. Terrifying stories of abduction and murders are rampant.

These versions of history have also made their way into the official educational curriculum. The Urdu book Adan refers to above, which depicts the picture of Sikhs butchering children with their swords, is a textbook endorsed for Class 5 by the Punjab Textbook Board, which falls under the government of Punjab. These books are studied widely across the province, both in private and public schools. Other provinces have their own education departments after the 18th Amendment to the constitution was passed, giving autonomy to the provinces. However, similar hate content makes its way in there too.

The National Commission for Justice & Peace (NCJP), which was established by the Catholic Bishops' Conference in Pakistan in the 1980s and serves as a body for human rights advocacy in the country, recently published a study called 'Education Vs Fanatic Literacy'. The study explores the hate content in textbooks in Punjab and Sindh and highlights the widespread biases in the system. According to the research, it is said, 'Indophobia and Anti-Hinduism were the driving factors behind the re-writing of school textbooks [in the late 1970s] in Pakistan in order to promote a biased and revisionist historiography of the subcontinent.'[10] Tariq Rahman, a renowned professor and researcher, further says: 'Pakistani textbooks cannot mention Hindus without calling them cunning, scheming, deceptive or something equally insulting.'[11]

---

[10]National Commission for Justice and Peace (NCJP). *Education Vs Fanatic Literacy.* (Sanjh Publications, March 2013), p.6.

[11]Ibid., p.7.

Many of Adan's teachers who grew up in the late 1980s and 1990s, must have studied from the same textbooks in school. I have personally also seen the term Hindu being used alongside words like mischief-makers and traitors. Mansoor Ahmad's (Chapter Thirteen) Hindu friends or the Sikhs that had saved Intikhab Alam (Chapter Seven) never make it to the textbooks. Instead, history is taught in a selective, censored manner. The script is written, directed, produced and sponsored by state authorities. The messages that are conveyed are politically motivated, aligned with the national ideology.

The slanted narrative reinforces the rationale for the country's existence; it creates a sense of patriotism in the Pakistanis. Their country is what prevented them from being subjected to the same treatment meted out to their parents and grandparents. She is what gave them freedom to practise their faith. She is what saved them. Thus, to be a Pakistani in a way means to be opposed to India, to see her as a lethal snake, one that can bite at any time, one that must be fought against consistently. For to fight it is to protect oneself from the torture that 'we' faced in our history. As part of this, bloated army budgets also become justified.

I ask Adan if I can sift through his textbooks so I can refresh my memories from my own school years. The books include a mix of private textbooks as well as the Punjab Textbook Board-endorsed books. While the private textbooks, endorsed by the Cambridge Board in the UK and taught to thousands of students who are enrolled in schools following the popular British educational system in Pakistan, can be said to be far less hardline, they too are not devoid of biases. In a recent conversation with the head of the Cambridge Board at a meeting in Islamabad, I inquired about this. He told me that the Pakistani government directed the board on what needed to be included in the Pakistan Studies syllabus and they had little freedom to challenge the biased rhetoric unless the request came from the government itself. Thus as I begin to flip through Adan's books, and later through the NCJP study, familiar depictions of Muslims being harassed by 'infidels' come my way in both sets of books.

'Hindus got enraged and started the genocide of Muslims . . . Englishmen were the ruler and Hindus were the enemy.' Class 9 & 10, *Essay Writing (Independence Day & Quaid-e-Azam)*, Urdu Grammar and Composition, 2012-2013 (Punjab Textbooks), pp.82-83[12]

'Hindu thugs started killing Muslims and burned their properties with the patronage of the government.' Class 8, *Political awareness of Muslims of South Asia*, Social Studies 2012-2013 (Punjab Textbooks), p.80[13]

'Hindus also harmed Muslims in every possible way,' Class 5, *Pakistan an Islamic Country*, Islamiyat 2012-2013 (Punjab Textbooks), p.45[14]

'Hindus can never become the true friends of Muslims,' Class 5, *Sir Syed Ahmad Khan*, Social Studies 2012-2013 (Punjab Textbooks), p.83[15]

'Whilst [the Congress Tyranny] was never an official Congress policy, Muslims feared that a major aim of their Hindu rivals was to erase Muslim culture . . . Muslims were forbidden to eat beef and received harsh punishments if they

[12] Ibid., p.13.
[13] Ibid., p.16.
[14] Ibid., p.17.
[15] Ibid., p.18.

slaughtered cows. *Azaan* was forbidden and attacks were carried out on mosques. Noisy processions were arranged near mosques at prayer times and pigs sometimes pushed into the mosques. Muslims felt that if they lodged complaints with the authorities decisions would always be taken against them. Sometimes there were anti-Muslim riots in which Muslims were attacked and their houses and property set on fire.' Nigel Kelly, *History and Culture of Pakistan*, Pakistan Studies, Class 9 & 10 (Peak Publishing UK, 2013), p.83

'The Wardha Scheme: An education scheme based on Gandhi's views . . . Teaching was to be in Hindi . . . All students were expected to bow before a picture of Gandhi hung in their schools. Muslims saw these measures as an attempt to subvert a love for Islam amongst their children and convert them to Hinduism.' Nigel Kelly, *History and Culture of Pakistan*, Pakistan Studies, Class 9 & 10 (Peak Publishing UK, 2013), p.83

It is well known that Islam, from its origin, has denounced idol worship and consumption of pork. To shove what is *haram* or forbidden into a sacred place of worship, would amount to an outrageous offence in any religion. In Islam, the *azaan*, or call for prayer from the mosque, forms an essential pillar of the faith. Muslims must pray five times a day, this is their duty. To be obstructed from performing this act or disrespecting the masjid is sacrilegious, to say the least. Similarly, bowing down in front of a picture in Islam would equate to *shirk* (idolatry), one of the biggest sins a Muslim—or a human being, for that matter—can commit, according to mainstream Islamic teachings.

These instances of blasphemy and disrespect may not be entirely fabricated. However, when such episodic events are promoted as the typical behaviour of 'them' without providing larger context and when most children are not introduced to other realities—the fact that many times Muslims instigated the attacks or that often people from the 'other' communities actually saved Muslims and vice versa, a rigid and distorted understanding of the 'other' takes birth.

The NCJP study shows that similar hate content is also present in textbooks in Sindh. A few glaring examples include:

'Since their belief and culture is different from non-Muslims, therefore cooperation with Hindus in any situation is impossible.' Class 9, *Pakistan Ideology*, Urdu 2012-2013, p.42[16]

'But as was their habit, Hindus deceived Muslims at every step.' Class 8, *Pakistan Ideology*, Social Studies 2012-2013, p.101[17]

Frighteningly enough, the report concludes that hate sentiment in both Punjab and Sindh textbooks is only increasing over the years. Conducting a comparison between textbooks used in 2009-2011 and 2012-2013, it notes that while in Punjab 'there were 45 lines of hate material in the syllabus books for 2009 . . . the number increased to 122 in 2012'.[18] Similarly, in Sindh in 2009 there were eleven chapters consisting of hate material; this had increased to twenty-two by 2012.[19]

In Khyber Pakhtunkhwa Province, too, this trend is being followed. While the provincial government led by the Awami National Party (ANP) had undertaken promising reforms post 2008, the new leadership spearheaded by the Pakistan

---

[16] Ibid., p.20.

[17] Ibid., p.21.

[18] Ibid., p.12.

[19] Ibid., p.19.

Tehreek-e-Insaf (PTI) has begun reversing the impact as of late 2013. The ANP government had removed some of the verses on jihad from the elementary and secondary school syllabus, as they were deemed unsuitable for consumption by young students. These verses are being reinserted while pictures of girls with uncovered heads and dresses are being deleted and any non-Muslim personalities that had been included—for example, the prominent Hindu ruler of Sindh and parts of Punjab, Raja Dahir—are being removed. According to Atif Khan, the provincial education minister, 'The previous government . . . had made some changes in the curriculum and removed sections from syllabus. Those changes didn't suit our Islamic society.'[20]

While textbooks are not the only source of information these children have—and fortunately for some, other experiences and narrations can be powerful in shaping more tolerant mindsets—they continue to play an instrumental role in moulding perceptions. As political scientist Stephen Cohen puts it, 'To tell lies to the school students, to relate fairy tales to the undergraduates, and to present fabrications in university lecture halls, is to sow an ill wind which will one day rise to a storm, disrupt society and endanger the state.'[21] This is a threat that Pakistan faces today. While many point towards madrassa education as promoting narrow-minded and

---

[20]Ahmad, Jibran, 'Pakistan province rewrites textbooks to satisfy Islamic conservatives', Reuters. Web: http://www.reuters.com/article/2014/10/30/us-pakistan-education-idUSKBN0IJ1G820141030 (Last accessed: 27 November 2014).

[21]Ahmed, Zahid Shahab, and Baxter, Michelle Antonette, *Attitude of Teachers in India and Pakistan: Texts and Contexts*, Women in Security, Conflict Management and Peace. (WISCOMP 2007), p.75.

extremist ideology, they are not the only platforms sowing the seeds of hatred. It is in fact mainstream schools—which target the majority of students—that are increasingly becoming tools of intolerance and are providing a distorted view of the other. Madrassa schools, in comparison, only target a minority of children.[22] While I have deliberately focused on textbook passages that target Hindus, similar descriptions for Jews and Christians are also widely present in government-endorsed textbooks. The result is fear, suspicion and mistrust; and in extreme cases, vengeful attacks against the 'other', which are becoming only too frequent both inside and outside of Pakistan.

Adan tells me that as he crossed over Wagah border with his friends for the Exchange-for-Change project in early 2012, he kept thinking back to his Class 5 Urdu book: 'What if the Sikhs saw us and tried to kill us just like they had butchered Muslim children at Partition? I almost expected them to be holding daggers,' he says, 'that's what most of my class fellows thought too. Many still do . . . those who haven't met any real Indians . . . many of them still hate them.'

Unfortunately, I have not been able to conduct extensive research in India and thus, cannot engage deeply with whether a similar reaction to Pakistan is being bred on the other side. However, from my own visits across the border, and from the minimal secondary research available, I have attempted to get a glimpse inside the country.

---

[22]For data on enrolment, please refer to: ASER Pakistan, *National Report 2013*. http://www.aserpakistan.org/document/aser/2013/reports/national/ASER_National_Report_2013.pdf (Last accessed: 27 November 2014).

The National Council of Educational Research and Training (NCERT) was set up in 1961 as an autonomous body by the government of India to assist the central and state governments on policies for improvement in the education system. Today, NCERT produces textbooks in English, Hindi and Urdu and these books are used as model textbooks for all schools affiliated with the All-India Central Board of Secondary Education (CBSE). Even schools that are not affiliated with CBSE often adapt or adopt the NCERT-prescribed, and government-endorsed, textbooks.

According to a research study published by Women in Security, Conflict Management and Peace (WISCOMP) in 2007, researchers Zahid Shahab Ahmed and Michelle Antonette Baxter argue that though the initial NCERT history books were written by some of India's renowned historians—Romila Thapar, Satish Chandra, Bipan Chandra, Ram Sharan Sharma—and displayed a progressive outlook, they were soon challenged by the Hindu Right. The early attempts to subvert the curriculum failed but by the late 1990s, the goal had largely been accomplished.[23] The saffronization process had begun.

Some slanted texts in the NCERT textbooks included:

'We are told that during the reign of Iltutmish, a party of Muslim divines approached the Sultan and asked him to enforce the Muslim law strictly, giving the Hindus the option of only Islam or death.' Medieval History—A History Textbook for Class XI, NCERT 2001, p.84.[24]

---

[23]Ahmed, Zahid Shahab and Baxter, Michelle Antonette, *Attitude of Teachers in India and Pakistan: Texts and Contexts*, Women in Security, Conflict Management and Peace. (WISCOMP 2007), pp.31-32.

[24]Ibid., p.35.

'A vehement persecution of the Brahmanas began in the reign of Sikandar Shah (1389-1413). The Sultan ordered all the Brahmanas and learned Hindus should become Musulmans or leave the valley. Their temples were to be destroyed and the idols of gold and silver to be melted down in order to be used as currency.' Medieval History—A History Textbook for Class XI, NCERT 2001, p.84.[25]

While some of the instances highlighted in the textbooks may have authenticity, for a fifteen- or sixteen-year-old child such episodes can often come to represent the only versions of the past. Fortunately, in India, the secular and left leaning forces came to the forefront to criticize the prejudiced overtones in the curriculum. The 2005 National Curriculum Framework encouraged a more holistic understanding of history and as a result, many positive steps have been undertaken. One such milestone is the chapter on Partition as part of the Themes of Indian History Part III Textbook (New Delhi, NCERT 2007). This chapter, written by Dr Anil Sethi, targets Class 12 students who opt for the arts after completing Class 10.

Dr Sethi employs the use of oral histories and external resources like Urvashi Butalia's The Other Side of Silence to present a holistic understanding of the events that led up to 1947 and the consequences faced by ordinary people. It starts off by documenting Partition experiences, including rescue stories. The first narration is set in Lahore in 1992; when a fellow Muslim treats a Sikh very well, the Sikh inquires about the reasons behind such kindness. In response, the Muslim tells him that during Partition an elderly Hindu woman had rescued

[25] Ibid.

his father and he wanted to return the favour. When the Sikh tells him that he isn't Hindu, the Muslim responds: 'I don't know what your religion is with any surety. You do not wear uncut hair and you are not a Muslim. So, for me, you are a Hindu and I do my little bit for you because a Hindu *mai* saved my father.' Another story narrates how a Sikh longed to meet a Punjabi speaking Muslim for several years and when he finally comes across one from Lahore, he becomes teary-eyed and embraces him. While a third example highlights the bitterness of Partition in that a Pakistani tells an Indian that they can never be friends for Indians wiped away his entire village in 1947, this is mentioned within the context of the brutality and loss of Partition rather than presented as the only sentiments that Indians and Pakistanis can project towards each other.[26]

However, though it is encouraging to see that the NCERT textbooks are not openly promoting animosity, by glossing over important details or censoring certain historical facts, especially in textbooks that are used up to grade 10, they too leave a historical vacuum to be usurped by biased media channels, mainstream propaganda and religious extremists. According to Krishna Kumar, author of *Pride and Prejudice: School Histories of the Freedom Struggle in India and Pakistan* (Penguin Books, 2002), 'the Indian narrative plays little attention to the course of post 1920s Muslim politics ... the pedagogic cost is that the 1940s must come as a surprise. Without the background of the social and political alienation of the Muslim landed elite and the intelligentsia of the northern plains, the

---

[26]Themes in Indian History III, Theme Fourteen, *Understanding Partition* (NCERT), pp.377-79.

student can hardly make sense of the sudden emergence of the Muslim League as a powerful actor in the early 1940s. Not surprisingly, the Indian narrative is extremely reluctant to go into the details of any event following Quit India. Textbooks jump from one mention to the next, rushing towards Partition which, from the point of view of the young student, begs for an explanation more substantial than what the British-Muslim conspiracy theory can provide . . . the Indian narrative of the national movement socializes the young to perceive Pakistan as an illegitimate achievement.'[27]

Unlike in Pakistan, where Partition is presented as a victory, in Indian textbooks it is expressed as a loss, and one with little justification for the ordinary student. Partition serves as the last major historical event and is likely to remain etched in students' minds. I found no references to the wars of 1965, 1971 or even the Kashmir issue as I viewed the online versions of the history books. They are left to the political science textbooks used in Class 12 by selective students. This is in deep contrast to the Pakistani state texts, where these events remain central.

While I do not propagate teaching children about wars and violence and feel that the omission of overt hate sentiment is a huge victory for those who have struggled against prejudiced teaching, it means that the missing links need to be filled in through other sources. Without an understanding of why and how the creation of Pakistan unravelled, without being aware of the historical realities that impact current relations between

---

[27]Kumar, Krishna, 'Peace with the Past', Web: http://www.india-seminar.com/2003/522/522%20krishna%20kumar.htm (Last Accessed: 12th January 2015).

India and Pakistan, and without having a grasp over the origins and unfolding of the Kashmir issue—a continued bone of contention between the two states—the young minds are left with the enormous task of piecing together the complicated puzzle of subcontinent's history with guess work and fragmented, and often censored, titbits. Their perception of the past and present in the context of Pakistan remains at risk of being myopic and flawed. Kumar states, 'as educated Indians, we have all been socialized to perceive the creation of Pakistan as an act of betrayal and narrow-mindedness; and now, more than half a century after that act was accomplished, we are led to believe that Pakistan is a failed state. While comparing ourselves to Pakistan, we take pride in having survived so far as a democracy, and especially as a secular democracy. The assumed points of our superiority are grounded in the coutours of our knowledge of history, particularly our knowledge of Partition and the decade preceding it.[28]

No wonder that on my trips to Indian schools, students often rushed to me to ask why I wasn't wearing a *burqa,* whether Pakistan had ATMs or Pizza Hut, whether all of us were fanatics. The absence of—coupled with minimal people-to-people contact—a holistic history allows media propaganda, filtered oral histories, political instability and terrorist attacks to dominate the thought process. The 2008 Mumbai attacks, the attack on the Indian parliament, the Kashmir conflict, the Mumbai riots are entrenched in students' minds. Just as in Pakistan Hindus have become synonymous with India— thereby Shahrukh Khan, being a Muslim, cannot be an Indian—in India, terrorism and Pakistan are increasingly

---

[28] Ibid.

becoming synonymous too. The result is a growing hatred and suspicion of Pakistan and the Ms (as I've sometimes heard Muslims being referred to in India), a sentiment only exacerbated by the Hindu Right whenever it gets the chance.

The WISCOMP study states: 'The Hindu right wing rejects secularism and argues that India's national identity is rooted in Hindu culture and civilization. Muslims and Pakistan are cast as the enemy of the *Hindu Rashtra* (Hindu nation). Pakistan is seen as the "foreign hand" supporting anti-India activities, responsible for all "terror" attacks against India. Thus any linkage with Pakistan is viewed as anti-national.'[29] Until now, the space for such thoughts is limited but the future remains uncertain.

On one of my recent trips, I visited a high-income school in the posh Matunga area of Mumbai as well as a low-income one in Dharavi, known to be the largest slum in Asia. In both schools, despite the vast class difference, the students were completely baffled by me. 'How come you are wearing jeans? How is your English so good? Have you seen the terrorist Hafiz Saeed?' As I struggled to answer these questions in a way that would present an accurate picture of Pakistan while clearing many of the misconceptions, a young child of no more than six years of age ran up to me. Holding up my visitor's tag, he asked, 'Visitor, visitor, where are you from?' When he was unable to guess, I finally gave in and told him 'Pakistan!' His eyes widened instantly and clutching his school bag across his chest, he turned on his heel and began to run. I yelled after

---

[29]Ahmed, Zahid Shahab, and Baxter, Michelle Antonette, *Attitudes of Teachers in Indian and Pakistan: Texts and Contexts.* Women in Security, Conflict Management and Peace (WISCOMP), p.23.

him and asked, 'What happened?' Looking back, he sheepishly said, 'I'm scared of Ajmal Kasab.' A child of such tender age had already made the equations in his head. Pakistani meant terrorist, fanatic, fundamentalist.

It was during this time—when I was running the Exchange-for-Change project and frequently conversing with students, mostly Pakistani but at times Indian, too—that I began to understand what Nandy meant by the 'packaged view' of violence and hostility the younger generations were exposed to. Many of these children had only been taught about the violence from the 'other' side, whether of Partition or of the recent decades of terrorism. In Pakistan, in particular, due to the limited number of minorities left in the country, Hindus and Sikhs just became figments of their imagination.

While media and other channels have played a critical role, I have been particularly intrigued with how oral history transmissions and mainstream school curriculum have been at the forefront of promoting a myopic understanding of Partition and the 'other' in Pakistan. One would assume that as we move further away from 1947, the horror stories would take a back seat, that we could let go of the bloodshed. But in reality, textbooks and the popular narrative in the country are ensuring that that does not happen. Instead, what goes 'missing' from texts and dialogues are the positive encounters the Partition generation might have had.

The brighter stories—for instance, stories recorded in Nandy's study on Partition about a significant proportion of people being saved from death at the hands of a mob by people from the 'other' community—have largely remained untold. In reviewing Nandy's work, writer Tridevish Singh Maini states that these stories 'were obscured by the larger tension and hatred'.[30]

This has been my personal experience as well, not just through school curriculum but also through the stories I heard from my grandmother, a witness to Partition. The oral histories I received from her became a source of linear understanding for me. For years, I only heard about how many bodies she had to bury at the refugee camp, how Sikhs and Hindus would tie women to separate ends of vehicles and stretch them apart till their bodies would tear. As a twenty-four year old at Partition, those gory memories remained central in her mind. In face of this, memories of her friends and neighbours seemed to pass us by. For the majority of my life, she never spoke of them but when I asked her if she had Hindu classfellows in her school, Rajeshwari and Uma began to intrude upon our usual Partition conversations. They were two of her closest friends, both of whom had to flee to India during Partition. It was not as if my grandmother did not remember them; they had been in touch for years afterwards. Rajeshwari had brought her Indian saris while my grandmother sent back *chikan karhai* suits with her, but she certainly had to be encouraged to recollect and share these stories.

During these conversations I also learnt that my grandmother's sister, Khala Cho, was in Amritsar when Partition was announced. Frantic about her safety, my great-grandfather had called upon his Sikh colleagues to give her refuge. He had obliged and had protected her as if she was their own until her family managed her rescue from the mainly

---

[30]Maini, Tridevish Singh, 'The Brighter Side of Midnight', *The Times of India*, 15 August 2010.

Sikh-dominated area to the safer Muslim territory. Needless
to say, they had put their life at risk to do so. Another
conversation revealed that my grandmother's other sister's pet
name, Guddi, was in fact kept after the daughter of her father's
Sikh friend. Amidst the calamity of Partition, such recollections
began to take a back seat and escaped the generations that
followed. They were subsumed by the metanarratives of
violence and displacement. My mother never knew about any
of these stories till I heard them from my grandmother. She,
too, had only heard about the massacres of 1947 till then.

However, while these memories were predominant in the
minds of many Partition survivors, and in turn in their children
and grandchildren, the silver lining was perhaps that many of
them did recollect a more nuanced past—either on their own
or through prodding and encouragement. When pushed,
memories that were deep-seated in the subconscious often
unfolded stories that had never been heard. It is these stories
that have the power of changing mindsets as they did in my
case. Adan tells me it was the same for his mother, Uqba.

When he was selected to go to India, Uqba forbade him
from doing so. She cried and told her husband that if he went,
he might never come back. Her father had lost most of his
family and property in Kapurthala at Partition. 'When they
came to Pakistan they were left with nothing so I had a very
frightening picture of India in my head,' she said, 'but when I
told my father that Adan had been selected to go to India, he
told me to let him go. He said he was confident that he would
be fine there. I was shocked that despite losing so much, he
still wanted to let his grandson go back. It made me rethink
that maybe India wasn't such a bad place . . .'

Today's children, however, are fast losing their access to
survivors of Partition. As we lose the Partition generation, the

chance of hearing this anecdote or that, of resurfacing of memories from the conscious or subconscious, are dwindling possibilities. The revision of the curriculum to present history in a one-sided way only exacerbates the filtered learning. Rather than moving on from Partition, for many children history is being reinterpreted as one in which Hindus and Sikhs are bad, Muslims are the purifiers of their infidel practices and India continues to only be an enemy. The diluted identities that people from the Partition generation experienced—for instance, Naseer Ashiq's (Chapter One) father, who was adopted by a Sikh family—or Shireen (Chapter Four) and Malik Siddiqui (Chapter Five), who have homes in both countries, have a shrinking space for these young Pakistanis. While for the Partition survivors like my grandmother, these realities had been pushed to the subconscious, for the youth, they are being wiped out from the collective conscious and subconscious memory altogether.

In India, too, though it continues to remain multicultural and host a large Muslim population, the post-Partition years have seen a crystallization of communal identities. With the rise of the Hindu Right, an otherization has started to take place, one that clearly defines Hindu, Christian and Muslim as opposite from the other as part of the nationalism process. The repercussions can be viewed in the communal fights, in violent episodes such as the Babri Masjid incident and the Gujarat riots. Or in everyday interactions when Pakistanis are refused accommodation in Indian hostels and hotels, or a seat in a taxi, simply due to their nationality and religion.

Just recently, an Indian friend of mine had been asked to stop talking to me when she expressed a desire to come to Lahore. Her in-laws were afraid of the intentions of her Pakistani friend. All Pakistanis are fanatics, they said.

EPILOGUE

I am sitting in the car with my husband Haroon. The windows are rolled down as we wait for warm plates of *naan cholay* to be delivered to us from the *dhaba* on our left. The *cholay* of Laxmi Chowk are famous across Lahore. The Chowk, once known for being the centre of the Pakistani film industry and the hub of entertainment, gets its name from the Laxmi Building that stands by our side. The façade, which was thought to have overt references to Hinduism, has recently been renovated to resemble the modern architecture across Lahore. It is a dismal attempt; the fresh blue paint looking tacky and out of place in the midst of the other yellowish buildings in the neighbourhood. Once this area had boasted of a rich Hindu community but today the handful that remain have receded to the back alleys. Most Pakistanis are unaware of their existence.

A young boy of no more than twelve years of age brings our order, stacked on a silver tray. He hands us our plates and throws pink napkins on the dashboard before rushing away to his next customer. Besides us there is a white Suzuki parked. A young girl with curly hair is resting her chin on her car window, looking out at the deserted blue façade. She turns to her brother and asks, '*bhai, woh kya hai?*' (brother, what is that?) He seems to be just a few years older than her. Taking one glance he shakes his head and goes back to toying with the gadget in his lap. In front, their mother is busy fumbling through her bag for change. Their father is scrolling down his phone. The girl stares at the building for a few more seconds before turning away. Her mother is asking her to sit straight so she doesn't spill her food. As Haroon and I pay our bill, the family of four also begins to hand back their plates. I turn to look at her as we reverse our car. She is busy cleaning her hands and taking out her colouring book from her school bag. She doesn't look up at the building again. The question that had arisen in her young mind had gone unanswered. Would she ever know the story behind Laxmi Chowk? Would she ever care to ask again? Would anyone ever tell her of the people, the homes and lives that flourished for years where we stand today? As the fourth or fifth generation living in Pakistan, is it even important for her to know?

From nearby, the *khutba* for the Friday prayers blares out of the mosque's speaker. The *khutba* takes place before Friday prayers every week as well as before the special Eid prayers twice a year. Its purpose is to guide Muslims upon the right path, though it is often used by ill-meaning religious extremists to promote hatred. The *maulvi* starts off by telling his audience that they must support their Muslim brothers around the world. Those suffering in Chechnya; those in Palestine and those in Kashmir. He tells them it is the duty of Muslims to fight against those who are against Islam; who are causing Muslims harm across the world. He tells them that now, more than ever, Muslims need to unite; against America, against India, against Israel, if we are to prosper. Then he tells them that Jews and Hindus are responsible for all our troubles.

I roll up my window as a whiff of dust catches my eyes. The

last line I hear is, '*Israel or Hindustan ko tabah kardo, woh sirf humare dushman hain. Tahreekh iski gawah hai!*' (Destroy India and Israel, they are only our enemies. History gives evidence of this!) We begin reversing our car to make our way out of the area. The girl and her family are heading out, too, their windows still rolled down. Soon shops will be closed for the prayer break. The same cycle will repeat next Friday.

REFERENCES

1. 1947 Archive, *About Partition.* Web: http://www.1947partition archive.org/?q=press_release
2. Ahmed, Ishtiaq, 'A Bloody March in 1947', *The News,* 18 August 2007 (print)
3. Ahmad, Jibran, 'Pakistan Province Rewrites Textbooks to Satisfy Islamic Conservatives' (Reuters). Web: http://www.reuters.com/article/2014/10/30/us-pakistan-education-idUSKBN0IJ1G820141030 (Last accessed: 27 November 2014)
4. Ahmed, Zahid Shahab, and Baxter, Michelle Antonette, *Attitude of Teachers in India and Pakistan: Texts and Contexts,* Women in Security, Conflict Management and Peace. (WISCOMP 2007)
5. ASER Pakistan. *National Report 2013.* Web:http://www.aser pakistan.org/document/aser/2013/reports/national/ASER_National_Report_2013.pdf (Last accessed: 27 November 2014)
6. Butalia, Urvashi, *The Other Side of Silence: Voices from the Partition of India,* Penguin Books, 1998
7. Butalia, Urvashi, 'Memory, Lived and Forgotten', *The Financial Express,* 1 April 2007
8. Dutt, Sagarika, and Bansal Alok, eds., *South Asian Security: 21st Century Discourses,* Routledge, 2013
9. Gandhi, Rajmohan, *Punjab: A History from Aurangzeb to Mountbatten,* Rupa Publications, 2013

10. Ghose, Sagarika, 'The Partition Psychosis'. Web: http://www.outlookindia.com/article/The-Partition-Psychosis/204034 (Last accessed: 24 November 2014)

11. Kaur, Ravinder, *Since 1947: Partition Narratives among Punjabi Migrants of Delhi*, Oxford University Press, 2007

12. Kelly, Nigel, *History and Culture of Pakistan*, Peak Publishing UK, 2013

13. Khan, Yasmin, *The Great Partition: The Making of India and Pakistan*, Yale University Press, 2007

14. Kumar, Krishna, 'Peace with the Past'. Web:http://www.india-seminar.com/2003/522/522%20krishna%20kumar.htm (Last accessed: 17 November 2014)

15. Maini, Tridevish, 'The Brighter Side of Midnight', *The Times of India*, 15 August 2010

16. Nandy, Ashis, *Pakistan's Latent 'Potentialities'*, Radio Open Source. Web: http://radioopensource.org/ashis-nandy-on-pakistans-latent-potentialities/ (Last accessed: 24 November 2014)

17. National Commission for Justice and Peace (NCJP), *Education Vs Fanatic Literacy*, (Sanjh Publications, 2013)

18. Sanhati, 'A Psychological Study of India's Partition, and Some Surprising Results'. Web: http://sanhati.com/articles/1299/ (Last accessed 24 November 2014)

19. *Themes in Indian History III*, Theme Fourteen, 'Understanding Partition', (NCERT)